The Manual of Creative Ideas for Real Estate And Paper

P. THORPE

ISBN-13: 978-0-9983947-1-8

The Manual of Creative Ideas For Real Estate and Paper

By

P. Thorpe

Published by Mind's Eye Media, Incorporated

First Edition, Copyright © 1991, E.C. Cobbett for P. Thorpe as *A Manual of Creative Ideas for Real Estate and Paper*

Second Edition, Copyright © 1993, JMF Funding as *A Manual of Creative Ideas for Real Estate and Paper*

Third Edition, Copyright ©1997, JMF Funding as *How to Make Money with Real Estate and Paper*

Fourth Edition, Copyright © 1999, JPJ Unlimited, *How to Make Money with Real Estate and Paper*

The author, publisher, and distributors expressly and specifically disclaim any liability, loss, risk, personal or otherwise, incurred as a consequence directly or indirectly of the use and application of any of the contents of this book. The reader should seek professional counsel wherever and whenever uncertainty arises.

Publisher: Mind's Eye Media, Incorporated
3228 Wood Thrush Dr., #123
Punta Gorda, FL 33950

AUTHOR'S NOTE

Introduction to the reprint of the original edition of *THE MANUAL OF CREATIVE IDEAS FOR REAL ESTATE AND PAPER*

December 30th, 2017

Dear Reader,

This reprint of the original edition of *The Manual of Creative Ideas for Real Estate and Paper* must be credited to the efforts and time of a dedicated few who knew the book's history and potential value.

A quarter of a century ago, I sat staring at a 256K computer's blank screen (for which I had traded a house lot,) pondering the challenge I had set for myself.

The challenge: to write the definitive manual on Real Estate and Paper for people who wanted to use real estate and paper to build a financial future for themselves.

And to do it in under two weeks.

I started typing and here it is...

Sincerely,

P. Thorpe

EDITOR'S NOTE:

The Manual of Creative Ideas for Real Estate and Paper has sold thousands of copies since it was first introduced to real estate investors at a meeting in Ocala, Florida late in 1991. The book was first published in early 1992, with pages printed out on continuous feed paper on a "daisy wheel" printer and three-hole punched by the author. It became known as "The Little Green Book" and sometimes "The Little Yellow Book" depending on the current edition.

The book went through many permutations, most of them unauthorized. That was due to the way it was sold and the author was paid. The author allowed a few investor group leaders around the country to print the book in bulk and pay him $3.00 per copy. Some paid. Others just took the book and reprinted without permission or payment. Along the way, changes were made, occasionally good or at least valid, sometimes just bizarre. One real estate group claimed to have the book on audio read by the author, which was a pretty big revelation to the author.

We have tried to keep this fifth edition of *The Manual of Creative Real Estate and Paper* as close to the original as possible, right down to using the same style of apostrophes and quotation marks. One major change was made to the Real Estate

Agreement. In the original version, each line was numbered so the author could refer to the line and give an explanation—a bit of overkill. In this edition, we have taken the line numbers out; the clauses are referenced and easy enough to find.

Some of the stuff is downright dated. Back in 1992, just about everything was offline. When the author says he has known someone for 15 years, add another 25. When you see things like "read the classifieds" just add in the word "online" and you will know to go to Craigslist, and For Sale By Owner and all those convenient online sites. The same goes for anything being mailed in or taken to the bank and deposited. And then think how lucky you are to be living in the here and now!

Personal computers were just getting popular at the time and the author certainly knew how convenient they would make an investor's recordkeeping. However, back in those early days, ALL CAPS did not indicate the author was YELLING. We have toned him down in a couple of spots to spare your 21st century ears.

While many things have changed, including laws and prices, it is gratifying to see how well the strategies, ideas, and principles of *The Manual of Creative Ideas Real Estate and Paper* have held up. This 25th Anniversary Edition brings the book and the author full circle.

Read it. Think about what you're reading. Then go out and APPLY these strategies.

CONTENTS

INTRODUCTION

"*If you think education is expensive, try ignorance.*"
(Saw the above on VW Bug bumper sticker, Beverly, Mass. in 1976)

Dear Reader,

Thank you for taking the time to read this manual. Hopefully it will add to your continuing education. The following pages of ideas and techniques for dealing in real estate and paper represent a lot of time and effort on my part, not only to learn and do what follows, but to get my experiences down on paper. I have been planning to write this manual for the past ten years, but somehow the project always wound up on the back burner. Well, here is the first edition. I hope you will take the time to see and think beyond the numbers in order to grasp the theories and to practice these ideas until they become second nature to you.

Everything covered in this manual is drawn from my personal experience unless otherwise noted. Whenever possible, I have given credit to those who taught me, guided me and showed me the way. To these mentors I am forever grateful.

Please be aware that I am not an attorney and have no formal legal training. I am not a C.P.A. and have no formal tax training. You will need special assistance from professionals in these fields. Seek their help and guidance on legal and tax matters to avoid the numerous pitfalls that are out there. I wish you all the success in the world. And remember—good ideas only work when you do.

Sincerely yours,

P. Thorpe

REAL ESTATE ACQUISITION

REAL ESTATE ACQUISITION

Why acquire real estate?

Because, real estate, when properly acquired and managed, provides capital appreciation, equity build up, cash flows, tax benefits and a hedge against inflation. Real estate, both land and improved, has a broad-based market place with many different values, uses and users. This country has a vast supply. The demand for real estate is always there at some price or terms by users, lenders, investors or speculators. Real estate is not as liquid as a savings account, but if you know your market place and a few techniques, real estate equities can be turned quite quickly into cash, cash flows and/or trade for other benefits you might need at the time. For me, it is the best investment opportunity around.

Having owned land, apartment buildings, commercial properties and single family houses, my preference is the latter. Of all the forms of real estate, the single family house seems to be the one with the most opportunities, the easiest to acquire and manage, and the one with the most liquidity. Also, the small size of a single family transaction is well within the means of most investors. Unlike apartment buildings, a single family portfolio is not subject to a rent strike. There are more than enough opportunities for each of us willing to learn and to do.

The key here is the "proper" acquisition. The following section will give you some ideas.

FINDING SINGLE FAMILY HOUSE OPPORTUNITIES

"If you're new to single family investing, look at one hundred houses for sale before you write your first offer," Jack Miller said. Having invested in hundreds of houses for decades and taught thousands of us how to invest in houses, he knows of what he speaks. Take Jack's advice. Drive around neighborhoods in your area that are clean, neat and reasonably priced. Look where you would feel comfortable owning a rental house. Jot down the address and telephone numbers on the FSBO (For Sale By Owner) signs. Knock on doors and start asking the owners questions. By taking the time to talk with one hundred sellers, you quickly will learn values in your market place and learn to recognize a good deal. You will become comfortable asking important questions about the property, the owners and their problems. Find out what the sellers would charge for rent. What are other properties renting for in the neighborhood? Talk with brokers about current sales and rentals. Become the most knowledgeable person in your chosen investment area of town. Until you are very experienced, stick to your local area. Buying houses in other states and all over the country may impress your friends, but wait until you have a problem a thousand miles away. It can be a very expensive lesson.

Let's assume you have take the time to learn your market place, talked with one hundred owners and have decided to begin investing in single family houses.

"Where do I begin?"

Since we are in the "profit" business, the place to start is distress ownership situations. That is where the profit is. The old adage holds true: "You make your profit when you buy, not when you sell." With some effort on your part, distressed owners can be found. Eventually, they will contact you but for now you must do the locating. You need a system for finding, tracking and cataloguing opportunities. Mine works well and it's simple. I use 3x5 cards.

Every day I cut out all the FSBO ads from the real estate section of my local paper and paste them on to a card. I copy the ad phone number in the upper left hand corner, the date in the upper right corner and the property address (when I get it) in the top center. My cards are filed by the first three digits of the telephone number behind a tab card which has the three numbers printed on the tab. Then I arrange all my 3x5 ad cards in order by the telephone number. This system lets me see if owners are changing their ads and just how long they have been marketing their property unsuccessfully. They may change the ad but they don't change the phone number. Also by reviewing my cards I am able to see who has stopped advertizing. This tells me they have sold the property, given up hope of ever selling, or they can no longer afford the ads. All this is important information in the quest of a good deal.

Another opportunity area in your classified ad section is the properties advertized for rent. Two types of owners place "for rent" ads: investors like you, who can be a great source of information if you can get them talking and people who are trying to rent their vacant home because they haven't been able to sell it. Here is a great chance for a lease/option or lease/contract. (More about these ideas later.) These ads get posted in my 3x5 box along with the "for sale" ads.

Other sources of single family opportunities are real estate brokers, door hangers requesting you be contacted if the owners wishes to sell or knows of someone who does, foreclosure notices, bank-owned properties (REOs), flyers on public bulletin boards, ads you place in your local newspaper (I have found that the "shopping-guide" type newspaper—the ones that get thrown on your lawn for free—seem to be a good source because the ad costs are cheaper.) Also, canvas subdivisions on foot, bicycle, or car to find FSBO signs and talk with people you meet in the neighborhood. Carry a business card or flyer with your phone number and the fact that you buy houses. The key here is to get the word to as many people as possible that you are in the single-family-house-buying business. Eventually your phone will not stop ringing and that is the object of these exercises.

Now that you have some sources of opportunities and your 3x5 card system in place, you are ready for your phone campaign. This telephone qualifying process is used to determine who is a highly motivated seller and who is not (and to save you gas). We want only **highly** motivated sellers. With experience you will develop your own questioning technique that really works for you. Let me give you some direction in creating your list of questions. In John Schaub's single-family-house-buying seminar, *Making It Big on Little Deals*, he uses a wonderful series of questions that really qualify the seller's situation (if the seller survives the 62 questions). Here is a sampling of John's telephone questions. Note that they are short, concise and geared to quickly understand the seller's situation, needs and motivation. For all 62 you'll have to attend his seminar.

TELEPHONE QUESTIONS

Hi, I'm calling about the house. Are you the owner?

I'm ______________________. I am an investor and saw your ad. I may be interested if you can make me a good deal.

If I buy your house this week, can you make me a good deal?

Why are you selling it?

What kind of loan do you have?

If you don't sell, will you move?

How did you arrive at your price?

Are any other homes for sale on your street?

If I could only pay part, how much cash would you need now?

Would you consider renting me the property?

Could we close in six months?

If I bought it, would you like to stay in the house and rent it from me? For how long? For how much?

SUMMARY REPORT

Strengths:

Weaknesses:

John has been acquiring, managing and lecturing about single family houses for investment longer than the fifteen years I have known him. He is the expert in the field. If you plan to pursue single family investments, I recommend you catch his seminar on investing in single family houses as soon as possible.

From the above sampling of John's questions, you can get a feel for the approach you need to take. The object is to learn everything you can about the physical aspects of the property, the owners' situation, their problem, their motivation to sell and what they are prepared to do to resolve the problem. With proper questioning, the seller will begin to realize just how serious his problem might be.

Start with questions about the property which are non-threatening and will help build rapport between the seller and you. You need to know its location, neighborhood, style, size, number of bedrooms, baths, appliances, garage, exterior, roof, heat and air conditioning systems, pool, water, sewer, and general condition of all of the above. Next, and equally as important, find out about the existing debt(s) structure, the taxes and insurance costs, any arrearage, and any other economic factors pertaining to the property. Move on to questions about the owners* situation and why they have decided to sell. Use short, direct questions requiring more than a yes or no answer.

Here are few of my directed questions:

* What brought about your situation?
* What have you done to resolve your situation?
* What are you doing to delay the foreclosure?
* Why have you rejected previous offers
* Who is advising you on this matter?
* What will you do if you don't sell your house?
* How much are you in arrears?
* If I brought the arrearage current and took over your payments, how much cash would you need to move? How soon could you move?
* How quickly could we close?
* I'm free this evening. When could you show me the house?

The phone questioning is strictly for ascertaining the property and the sellers' situation and motivation. Do not hesitate to ask any question that will lead to more information. The better you understanding the sellers' situation the better offer you will write.

MAKE AN OFFER

Motivated sellers are selling because their situation is changing rapidly for the worse for any number of reasons. They are highly motivated to act now to solve their problem. Learn to find out exactly why they are selling and what their bottom-line needs are. From your phone questions you should have a firm grasp of their situation and problem. Tailor your offer to meet just those needs and no more. Be absolutely certain you can perform on what you have offered. (You will hear all kinds of sad stories; this is the time for action, not charity). Remember, always write your best offer. You will be surprised how often they are accepted or reasonably countered.

There are as many ways to make an offer as there are sellers. Offers can be structured in numerous ways depending upon the sellers' motivation and your abilities to perform. Let's talk about a few approaches to offers.

ALL CASH FOR THE PROPERTY - Cash really does talk. A friend in Texas told me the other day about a brand new residence he purchased last year for $175,000 ALL CASH. It was listed for $495,000. The builder/seller or his banker was highly motivated to get out of title to this 4,000+ sq. ft. custom house. After living there for a year or so the property has been resold for a $150,000 profit and my friend is looking for another residence. The numbers are large; but the concept should be clear: cash gets action. As a footnote, remember: Your home is a single family investment. It is better to live in a "good deal" rather than the ideal house with huge monthly payments.

Not all of us have anything close to $175,000 in ready cash. But there are lots of investors who do have money. And for the right deal they would gladly put up $20,000 or $50,000, provided you do all the work from start to finish and the investor is certain he will get his money back first. Then split the profits 50/50 or any other way acceptable to both of you. Small pension funds will loan against real estate using a mortgage or deed of trust and be very comfortable with monthly payments. The key to "all cash" is being certain that you have acquired the property at deep, deep discount and that you have access to the necessary cash. You make your profit when you buy, not when you sell.

Another source of all cash houses is banks holding foreclosed properties. Get to know your local banker and see what REOs (Real Estate Owned) he might have in inventory. He might be in a ready position to unload a house or two for less cash than he has in them. You will never know without asking.

SELLER FINANCING: Today many transactions involve seller financing where the seller holds paper for part or all of the equity. As a buyer, the trick here is to get the "softest" terms possible. One technique is "Interest Only" with the balance (balloon) due sometime in the future. Be careful about having too many balloons on a number of different properties all coming due at the same time. You will find yourself in a real fire drill in a hurry. Try to structure an escape mechanism in the balloon, such as "bubbles" where you can extend the balance for an additional period of time by making a small payment at the due date of the balloon. This small payment will buy you time to get your ducks in a row and avert a liquidity crisis.

In a number of cases you will be able to write your contract in such a manner as to create a "principal-only" loan. For example, take an absentee seller with a $50,000 free and clear house who is motivated to sell. With $3,000 down, offer to pay the balance ($47,000) with payment of $470.00 per month for 100 months. Now you have a principal only loan. Here's a great idea to use if the seller counters: "Fine, for every dollar of cash you want down, I'll have to reduce the price by $2.00." More on principal only loans will be coming up later.

OPTIONS: In 1978, Jack Miller introduced me to the power of real estate options in his seminar on options. Investing in single family houses suddenly got a lot simpler. Options eliminate management, lower the necessary investment cash, reduce the "at-risk factor" to only the amount of the option consideration, present no liability exposure, remove any need for commercial lenders, step over due-on-sale clauses, allow for real estate appreciation, capture the amortization of the existing debt, give tremendous leverage for greater profit with no down side, and allow more freedom and capital to do more deals than previously possible. Now you can see why options grabbed my undivided attention. One way or another options became part of my daily life.

An option contract says that one side of a transaction (the Optionor) has sold, leased, transferred ownership or divested himself completely of an asset, subject to the other side (the Optionee) making up his mind to accept or reject the contract sometime in the future, when and if he ever gets around to it. That's right. The optionee can decide to exercise or abandon the option at his leisure without suffering any liability. The optionee's only loss would be any option consideration he might have paid to acquire the option in the first place. The option is a powerful tool.

One dollar was the first option consideration I ever paid. It was for the right to buy a foreclosed single-family-house lot owned by a Salem, Massachusetts bank. After some homework (8 hours) and a land survey ($250), I sold my option for $3,000. I was hooked on options and went after bigger fish.

In North Carolina for $100 I acquired a 120-day option to purchase 15 just-completed single family houses from a financially strapped construction company for $32,000 each (which would just about pay off the company's lender). The houses had a market value of $50,000; but there was no market for the value. The construction company understood building, not marketing. The next day I traded my option position to a local single-family investor for an option position on each house. Within 90 days fifteen houses were sold for $49,900 each by using my equity participation formula. I controlled 25% ($4,475) of the equity in each of the houses with my fifteen options for a total position of $67,125 and I had no liability to anyone. By now you should begin to see the power of options.

LEASE/OPTIONS: One common technique of optioning is to put an option with a lease—the Lease/Option. This a powerful combination which can readily be used in acquiring real estate as well as divesting. When you acquire with a lease/option be sure to use two separate documents, a lease and an option. The reason for creating two documents is to give you flexibility in the future. Should you decide to go out of title to the option you will still have the lease. And vice versa. Be sure that the lease runs as long as the option. Get as long an option period as possible with as many rights to extend as possible. Have the title run to see exactly what is on record before you close your deal. Be sure to record a notice of contract (not the option itself) in the county registry of deeds to prevent any title problems. Also, get a signed and notarized deed from the other side placed in escrow with escrow instructions specifying exactly how, when and to whom the deed is to be passed.(Seek legal counsel on help with escrowed deeds.) The object in all this is to make certain that what has been contracted to happen will be done without a hitch when and if you should decide to exercise your option. In the option contract be sure that the optionor agrees to make all necessary payments, maintain the property and keep the place insured.

When acquiring with an option always establish the value of the property today. (let's say $50,000.) Agree on the option consideration to be paid now (say $2,000) which is to be counted as part of the total consideration. Establish exactly what is owed to any secured lender(s) and that they are current (say $36,000). Next subtract the total debt from the agreed-upon price to determine the exact equity presently in the property (for our example, the equity today would be exactly $14,000). Write your option contract to specify that when you exercise the option you will owe $12,000 to complete the contract and have the deed recorded. (Review the mathematics: $50,000 value today minus $36,000 existing debt today equals $14,000 equity today minus $2,000 option consideration paid today by you equals a balance due at strike time of $12,000. Why do it this way? Because now you have captured all of the amortization of the existing loans as well as the appreciation. Of course, you do the opposite of the above when you are the seller of the property. Options can be even more powerful than they appear at first glance.

CONTRACTS: One of the finest and subtlest lease/option type contracts I have ever seen was given to me by Pete Fortunato. Although he has been one of my closest friends and partner in numerous real estate and paper transactions over the past two decades, his brilliance and creativity never cease to amaze me. In 1985 he sent me one of his contract formats which he changes slightly to fit each deal. The following Agreement is his creation and his alone. With his permission it is:

AGREEMENT

Parties: ______________________________________ heirs, successors and assigns as Seller, of

____

And P. Thorpe of ______________________________, Florida, his heirs, successors and assigns

WITNESSETH: That Seller, in consideration of the payments, covenants, agreements and conditions herein contained which on the part of the buyer are to be made, done, and performed has this day sold, upon conditions hereinafter recited, to the Buyer the real property legally described as follows:

The street address of the property being conveyed is:

TERMS of this contract are:

1. Buyer will pay to Seller the sum of $_________ on the 1st day of each month commencing on _______________, 1992 and continuing until legal title transfers to Buyer or until _______________, whichever comes first.

2. On or before _________________, Buyer will pay to Seller the sum of $__________ in the following manner:

A. Cash when legal title transfers $______

B. Purchase money note and mortgage $______

C. The property is encumbered by mortgages with a current balance included in the total due, which Buyer may take title subject to, which has a balance not exceeding $___________

D. Total due Seller when title transfers $___________

3. ________ of each payment made by the Buyer pursuant to "1" above will be credited to the cash owed to the Seller when legal title transfers.

4. Exclusive occupancy and possession of the property transfer to the Buyer with the first payment made to the Seller under "1" above and remain with the Buyer until ___________ unless Buyer defaults on any payment required by this contract. A

default shall occur should any payment fail to be made within 15 days of the date it is due.

5. Should Buyer default on any payment required by this contract, all of the Buyer's rights to occupancy, possession and equitable title shall revert to Seller and all monies paid to Seller shall be retained by Seller as sole liquidated damages.

6. Buyer and Seller agree to fully execute and place in escrow with ________________________ Title Company all instruments required to convey this property. The Seller shall deposit a Warranty Deed, copies of existing notes and mortgages, survey, property and title insurance policies. The Buyer shall deposit a quit claim deed which shall be delivered to Seller in the event that the Buyer should default under this contract. The deeds, estoppels letters from mortgagee(s), closing statements and escrow instructions shall be fully executed as required to enable the transfer to be completed.

7. Seller shall keep the property improvements insured by a company acceptable to the Buyer for its full insurable value during the term of this agreement. Buyer shall be responsible for all costs of maintenance and repairs to the property not covered by the above insurance during the terms of this agreement.

8. All fixtures and articles of personal property attached or appurtenanced to, or used in connection with the property are, to the extent that they may be present on the premises when possession and occupancy transfer, subject to this contract. All fixtures, furniture, appliances and functional systems within the property will be delivered in fully functional operational condition.

CONVEYANCE: If Buyer shall notify Seller or Escrow Agent within the time above limited of the Buyer's intent to take legal title to the property, within 10 days of receipt of such notice, Seller will deliver fee simple title to the Buyer, or the Buyer's assigns, by those of record this date, which Buyer may take title subject to. Seller warrants that the existing mortgage(s) will be current in all payments of principal, interest and escrow amounts required by the mortgage(s) when legal title transfers. Seller shall not further encumber the property after the date of this contract and this contract may be recorded at the Buyer's expense putting the Public on notice that the closing of this contract will extinguish liens and encumbrances recorded after this contract. In the event of a foreclosure or bankruptcy of the Seller, the Seller's rights of redemption shall transfer to the Buyer without further compensation and this contract shall serve as conveyance without further notice or action.

SPECIAL PROVISIONS: No agreements, unless incorporated herein, shall be binding upon the Buyer or the Seller. There shall be no prorations or adjustments upon transfer of possession or transfer of legal title. This instrument shall become effective as a contract when signed by both Buyer and Seller. If not signed by both parties before ________________, 1992 this instrument shall be void. This contract is contingent upon inspection and approval of the property by the Buyer prior to transfer of possession.

THIS CONTRACT IS LEGALLY BINDING: IF NOT FULLY UNDERSTOOD, SEEK LEGAL ADVICE BEFORE SIGNING!

Signed, sealed and delivered this _____ day of __________, 1992

____

____

Witness Buyer

ACCEPTED, signed, sealed and delivered this ______ day of ________, 1992

________________________ ________________________

Witness Seller

________________________ ________________________

Witness Seller

STATE OF FLORIDA

COUNTY OF ______________________

The foregoing instrument was acknowledged before me this _____ day of _______________, 1992 by _____________________________, Seller(s).

Witness my hand and official seal.

____

Notary Public
My commission expires:

(Reprinted by permission of Peter F. Fortunato.)

Reread this agreement a couple of times. Pete has put some real power into this contract.

Pete's contract has the following effects. It is an offer to purchase real estate, a contract to purchase the property (with a principal-only loan), a lease to rent the property, and a real estate option all wrapped into one recordable instrument. In order to understand it better, make a copy and get a hi-lighter to accent the more important points. OK? Ready?

Let's take it a step at a time.

As an offer to purchase real estate from a buyer to a seller, the filled-out contract tells the seller when, how and what he is being offered for his property, (in the **SPECIAL PROVISIONS** clause on page 2 of the Agreement), the time-frame for acceptance is established. Beyond that point in time the offer is null and void. When the seller accepts the offer by signing and notarization (the Signature section at the end of the Agreement), a contract is born. It is binding on both parties and recordable. Both parties have some responsibilities (as spelled out in Item #6 of the **TERMS** section) to complete before the contract can stand by itself. The contract is also a bill of sale and warrantee (Item #8 of the **TERMS** section) for all the personal property and appliances included in the sale. All the described, necessary documents are completed and placed in escrow with a reputable title company. Upon completion of the escrow work, possession is handed over to the buyer.

At this point in time the document becomes a lease. The buyer has agreed to make monthly payments (Item #1 of the **TERMS** section) to the seller until the conclusion of the contract. The buyer has the right to live in (by making payments out of his own monies) or rent the property to a third-party tenant (buyer collects rent from which he makes his payments required under the terms of the contract). Interestingly enough, you will note (**TERMS** clause, Item #7, first line) the seller must still pay the insurance as well as the taxes and any underlying debt. The buyer is in a strong position, which was Pete's intent in the first place.

The buyer's position gets better. At this point the contract becomes an option to purchase real estate (Item #5 of the **TERMS** clause) because this paragraph limits the buyer's liability solely to any consideration already paid and no more. So if the buyer wishes to abandon his option he just stops making payments. The seller merely needs to instruct the escrow company to record the escrowed quit claim deed (Item #6 of the **TERMS** clause) in favor of the seller. Thereby the contract is completed and the seller has his property back. Very neat and clean.

Thus far, you have in your hands an offer to purchase real estate, a contract to purchase real estate, a lease of real estate with the right to sublet, a bill of sale and warrantee of personal property, and an option to purchase real estate. Still it gets better.

Remember the monthly payment the buyer has contracted to pay to the seller? Well, Item #3 of the **TERMS** clause starts off with a blank space. Put in "100%" and you will see what this does. It causes ALL OF THOSE MONTHLY PAYMENTS to be credited to what the buyer owes the seller on the note and mortgage (Item #2B of the **TERMS** clause) when the buyer decides to fulfill the terms of the contract and have the escrowed warranty deed recorded. The effect of this is make each payment paid a payment of principal only. And there you have your principal-only loan built into the contract.

Another point to note. If there is an existing amortizing loan owed by the seller at the time the contract is signed, the seller must continue to make the monthly payments out of the monthly payments he receives from the buyer. If this should happen to be a five or ten year contract, a great deal of amortization will have occurred. You will notice (Item #2C of the **TERMS** clause) that the seller has agreed to allow the buyer to take title "subject to" any existing debt (which of course is amortizing over time). The buyer has contracted to purchase only the existing equity at the time of the contract's inception. He has not contracted to pay a specific purchase price. Because of this, all the buyer owes the seller is the balance of the original equity. Therefore, all the amortization of existing debt belongs to the buyer.

A couple of final points for now. Under the **CONVEYANCE** clause, by recording this

Agreement, the title of the property is protected from any future liens, judgments or encumbrances. And, in the event the seller should have a foreclosure or bankruptcy, the seller has already transferred his right of redemption to the buyer as well as title to the property without need of any further compensation.

Life is so simple—until you read one of Pete's contracts. This Agreement takes some getting used to and I recommend that you review it carefully a number of times before heading out to use it with the public.

"A DISTRESS PURCHASE IN STAGES."

A friend of mine, [the late] Bobby Rock, in Northern Virginia taught me the following acquisition method which he has mastered and works to perfection. The concept is easy. Place an ad that lets distressed house owners know you buy single family houses. The ad he gave me reads, "NEED CASH? BEHIND IN YOUR HOUSE PAYMENTS? PRIVATE INVESTOR BUYS HOUSES. CALL...." When the phone call comes, use your counseling questions to determine just what and how big the problem really is. A typical situation is the owners are three months behind in their payments on their first (and second and third) mortgage with no hope of finding enough money to correct the arrearage.

After determining the property is one you might like to own and you have enough capital to bring the loans current, go view the property and meet with the owners. Make certain all those in title are present or you are wasting your time. If everything meets your criteria and you feel there is enough equity to protect your position, offer to bring all the back payments current in return for one half ownership of the property. They can stay in the house and pay to you all the mortgage, tax, and insurance payments that they were paying originally. You, in turn, will make the payments on time to the lenders. Of course all this is subject to a title inspection, estoppel letters from the lenders and perhaps a building inspection by a certified property inspector (all paid for by you). Let's assume everything is checked out and proves to be what you expected. You decide to proceed. So far so good.

I use a Grantor Deed To Trustee (my lawyer is trustee) and set up a Land Trust in which the owners and I now each own a one-half undivided interest in the trust—the sole asset of the trust being that specific property. The original owners sign a lease to me secured by their one half interest in the Trust. (Seek out a top-notch lawyer in your area for counsel before you do this. There are lots of rules and places for error). Everything is signed, sealed and notarized. The Grantor Deed is recorded and everyone's life goes back to normal.

Normal, at least for awhile. Payments come in on time for six months or so and of course you are making the necessary loan payments a day early. However, the payments to you slow down and eventually become sporadic. The people are in trouble again. After a meeting with them to analyze their situation, it mutually is decide to reduce their monthly payment to you by twenty five percent of their old payments. They agree that they can handle this new arrangement. In return for reducing their payments as well as having made a number of necessary loan payments out of your own pocket, they assign over to you their interest in the trust. Now they are tenants and you own the house outright, subject to the existing debts.

Time moves on and the rent to you falls behind. Sound familiar? It is now time for the eviction process. There are two schools of thought on this. Vinegar or Sugar. We'll talk a bit about both in the next section on HOLDING REAL ESTATE. When the ex-owner/tenants have moved from the property, it is 100% yours to repair, re-rent, and hold for investment.

The above scenario may seem tough or harsh. It is the real world. We have saved them two times and in some cases three times. If they cannot get their act together by now there is not a lot of hope for them down the road. Also remember they came to us because everyone else they turned to refused to help. I know a number of cases where the trust arrangement has helped buy home owners time to regroup and get on their feet again. They still have one half ownership of the trust. Both they and the investor are happy. In a few cases the one-half owner/occupants recovered enough to buy out the investor.

The object of the game is acquire real estate for profit, growth and cash flows. If you lose sight of this, you are in the wrong game.

ADDITIONAL IDEAS AND HINTS TO GET YOU THINKING

* Learn to say No. If something about a deal just isn't right, say "No" and move on.
* "Don't tell me want you won't do; tell me what you will do!" says Dee Fountain of Oregon.
* Always read each document all the way through and reread until you understand just what it says.
* Be sure to do your homework first and always.
* Always work off updated check lists. As deals get more complex, details get overlooked sometimes.
* Stick to questions and learn to listen to the answers.
* Set realistic goals for you to work towards and don't be afraid to change them as your needs change.
* Develop a game plan for reaching your goals.
* Always be a seeker of more knowledge. Push yourself into continuing your education.
* Keep a positive attitude. Life gets a lot easier fast.
* Enjoy life and spread the happiness around. There too many unhappy people already.

* "Think Time" - Use an hour each day to be alone and just think. Amazing what a powerful tool a cleared head can become.
* Get a small notebook, pad or 3x5 cards to jot down thoughts and ideas that hit you from time to time.
* Organize your day, week, year, life. I'm amazed at how much time gets wasted due to a lack of organization.
* Set up a daily routine that gets the most done with the least amount of effort. I use a 3x5 card with one project or deal to a card. I can shuffle them into a "need-to-be-done order," add developments to them when necessary and discard or file them when I'm done. Items posted in calendar books tend to be forgotten after a few days.
* Put the detestable, priority stuff first in your daily scheduling. Save the things you love to do for last. Kind of a built-in reward system.
* Reward and pat yourself on the back for a job well done. No one else will.
* When I have a real stumper of a problem, I will take a long walk on a beach or up a mountain. Somehow when I'm back, the solution has begun to take shape.
* Take a vacation once in awhile—when you've earned it.

* Take a public speaking course (or join Toastmasters). Amazing the self confidence you gain which really helps in your day to day relationships with others.
* When you have the details of a deal, practice writing as many different offers you can think of.
* Find a friend with similar interest and practice "Idea Tracking."
* Make an Idea Tracking list: Start with some of the ideas in this manual. I use photocopies of the Tables of Content from all the workbooks of seminars I have attended.

Now that you have acquired title or are in contract title of a single family house, the holding period begins (otherwise known as "management.")

REAL ESTATE HOLDING

REAL ESTATE HOLDING

Twenty five years ago, with a portfolio of apartment buildings, I learned multi-family management by the "trial and terror" method. With so many buildings and tenants and so much going wrong each day, I never seemed to be able to catch up, never mind get ahead. I made every mistake in the book and probably invented a few as well. It was management by crisis rather than management by objective. The four year real estate management experience taught me a great deal. But the most important thing I learned was "there has to be a better way."

There is a better way. Years after my apartment buildings had been sold, I heard John Schaub lecturing. He said, "You don't manage real estate; you manage people." The light went on. (Where was he when I needed him??) John went on to explain numerous ways to find, qualify and motivate tenants to behave themselves and not to bother the landlord. By then, he had my undivided attention. It became clear to me that if I could reduce management to a minimum, I could own more properties and have a lot more free time for other things. The ideas and tips that follow come from my own experience and the experiences of others kind enough to share them with me.

THE PROPERTY YOU WISH TO RENT. I shall be brief and to the point. The better the condition of the property (inside and out), the better the tenant and the fewer the problems down the road. If it needs work, do it NOW before you even consider looking for a tenant. If you have done your homework during the acquisition stage, you know exactly what needs to be repaired, how much it will cost, how long to complete and who is going to do it. Enough said.

FINDING THE PROSPECTIVE TENANT. Ads in your local classifieds work if you describe property, its location, the amount of the rent, a phone number other than your private home phone, and the sentence, "Be sure to ask about our Discount Rent Program." The latter will get you lots of calls and interested parties. (More about the Discount Rent Program in a minute). Also, I have used flyers about the rental handed out in the neighborhood. The neighbors tend to refer people they would like to have as neighbors.

In North Carolina, I found two good sources of tenants. The first was the numerous employers in the Research Triangle Park. Each company had its own relocation department. They proved very helpful in providing tenants who were being transferred into the area as well as putting notices out to their employees about available housing. The second source was a group of real estate investors which met monthly to discuss opportunities and problems with each other. Soon we were sharing tenant leads.

Signs work. I put the number of bedrooms and baths at the bottom of the sign. Anyone who calls on the "For Rent" sign has seen the outside of the property, the neighborhood and probably talked with some of the neighbors. They like what they have seen thus far and are close to making a decision. They would like to be shown the inside.

I tell them it is not company policy to show houses. They must come to the office to pick up the key, leave a $35.00 key deposit, view the house by themselves and return the key to the office for the refund of the deposit. (A photocopy of their drivers license is always made.) I have had people drive for over an hour each way to pick up and return the key. This is just one more step in the qualifying process.

As a footnote: It is extremely unwise to use this key deposit system if the house is presently rented.

QUALIFYING THE PROSPECTIVE TENANT. Your goal now is to acquire the "IDEAL TENANT."

The ideal tenant is the family who thinks of the house as their "home" not a "house" that they "rent." They will have the means to afford all the monthly costs associated with "home ownership." They are responsible and concerned about their good credit and their image in the community. The ideal family has a "pride of ownership" even though their circumstances do not warrant ownership at this time.

By stating the rental amount and the security in your for rent ad you have taken the first step of qualifying the prospective tenant. They know what it will cost per month.

The location and type of single family house you are offering is a most critical aspect of the qualifying process. I have talked with hundreds of S/F investors over the past twenty years about their successes and their failures in managing rental houses. John Schaub's description of the ideal rental house seems the best thus far. He told me, "A 3/2 with a two-car garage (attached), without a pool, in a middle class subdivision where all the house are neat and clean and my property is the only rental on the block, is what I've found to be Ideal." Reviewing my own trials and terrors in S/Fs, I think he is right.

If your property is run down and in a tough area, you will attract run down and tough applicants. (I would rather have one rental house in John's type neighborhood than four cheapies in the wrong location with all kinds of problems.) The reverse is true. The better the impression your property makes the better quality tenant you will attract.

The best way to qualify anyone for anything is a one-on-one meeting with all involved parties present. Your skills at counseling will be very helpful. I never tell the prospective tenants (or anyone else, for that matter) that I am the owner. I'm just the manager hired to manage the property. Next, in the qualifying process, is the RENTAL APPLICATION form. This asks for all the basic information about the applicant and any other applicants who intend to live in your house—the more information the better. My form has a separate signature place for the tenant to authorize a credit report. Develop your own application form (a good place to get most of what you will need is a bank loan application). After a lot of questions and answers on both sides, you will gain a sense of whether or not the applicants are what you are looking for. You inform them that you will contact them by phone once you have confirmed the information they have provided and after you have met with other tenant applicants. When you are satisfied with all your findings and a comfortable with your feelings about the applicants, schedule a second meeting to review and sign the lease.

THE LEASE: Remember, you manage people, not real estate. Your lease and how well the tenants understand it before signing will determine how few problems you will have. The object of any lease is to define who is responsible for what and when. Don't be afraid of a lengthy lease. Seven pages, single-spaced, is not unusual. There are five critical keys: The lease must cover every conceivable responsibility and contingency clearly; it MUST be legal; you must go over the entire document, reading it word by word out loud, with all those who will be signing present; you never change one word of the lease or make any exceptions for any reason (give an inch and you'll only give more); and you never allow anyone to take an "unsigned" lease out of your office.

Because the laws on landlord/tenant relationships vary greatly from state to state, county to county and city to city, you must seek competent legal counsel. It would be wise to have you CPA review it, too. It is not the intent of this manual to cover in detail the inner workings of some of the better leasing techniques, but let me cover some of the high points.

People are motivated with incentives and rewards, not punishment. By offering discounted rent for payments received by noon on the 1st, I find most people are happy to pay on time or early.

My "self-insurance" program is an incentive to keep equipment and appliances working. I offer to discount the rent again if they will pay for all repairs up to a certain dollar amount. Tenants seem to take better care of things when it is their responsibility.

Also, in North Carolina, I started my pay-by-credit-card plan. In the lease contract there is a paragraph specifically stating that they have authorized me, in advance, to use their credit card accounts (all necessary information is added to the lease), to pay the rent in full should they call the office and tell me to do so. It also authorizes me to charge the rent against their credit card account should the payment not be received within five days of the due date. Once I had a tenant leave unannounced and slightly behind in his payments. The credit-card-payment-plan was very helpful in bringing him current.

I offer the Christmas plan and a number of people have joined over the years. Take the gross annual rent, divide by ELEVEN months instead of twelve. This gives the tenant the twelfth month rent free which is December, if the lease begins on January 1st. This is great for tenant vacation planning also.

Second only to uncontrolled running water, pets will destroy a house faster than anything else. I prefer no pets. But if "Fifi" is really that important a member of the family, far be it from me to break up any working relationship. The pet deposit is bigger than the rent deposit. The cost per month for "Fifi" is a 20% rental increase. Sorry no exceptions to this company rule: "See, it says so right here in the lease contract you have in your hand." The applicants decide to try another landlord, agree to pay the required pet rent, or decide "Fifi" would really be much happier with the relatives back home.

The lease should recommend the tenants get their own tenants-contents insurance policy and warn of the consequences for failure to do so. As a landlord you should consider talking with your knowledgeable insurance agent about umbrella policies for liability. A five million dollar umbrella policy is cheap and will let you sleep at night.

Another clause in my lease is the "Good Neighbor Policy." This paragraph was inserted by me a long time ago to ensure that the tenants realize up front that they will be subject to immediate eviction if their life style, their "pets," their actions or those of their guests in anyway disrupts the neighborhood. Make this clause as strong as the law will allow. It tends to keep things fairly quiet. Firearms, fireworks or explosives of any type are not allowed under any circumstance.

A final concern before we move on. There are some real horror stories about improperly stored chemicals that have leaked onto the ground and then seeped into the water table. I have inserted a large paragraph pertaining to the tenants' responsibilities and liabilities pertaining to the storage, leakage, or disposal of any EPA regulated substance. AT NO TIME WILL THERE EVER BE ANY OF THESE SUBSTANCES ON OR ABOUT THE PROPERTY FOR ANY REASON WHATSOEVER. The EPA has a policy of suing the owner of record regardless of who, how or when the pollution damage was done. SO BE CAREFUL before you buy real estate, when you lease real estate to a tenant, or should anyone ever offer you a deed in lieu of foreclosure on a note he owes you. If you haven't thoroughly checked out the physical property, put everything on hold until you can have it inspected by experts in the field.

OTHER NECESSARY DOCUMENTS: Here are a few more instruments to keep things straight between you and your tenants.

* Key deposit receipt - refundable at end of lease term with return of all keys. Be sure to change the locks each time a tenant moves out.
* Inspection agreement - both the tenant and you have done a "walk-through" of the property to verify that everything is correct, in working order, and is in good condition. There will be another walk-through at the termination of the lease before any deposits are refunded.
* A list of local emergency telephone numbers - Fire, Police, etc. but I include an emergency number through which I can be reached. Otherwise my office hours are 9 to 5, Monday through Friday.

RECORD KEEPING: In a nut shell my record keeping system is the KISS formula - Keep It Simple (accurate and current) Stupid. I have always instructed the tenants in the lease to mail their monthly rental payments three days early to a specific account at the specified bank. The tenant understands that the rent with the deposit slip filled out MUST BE MAILED and not hand delivered for the system to work properly. At the lease signing I give the tenant twelve deposit slips and twelve prepaid self addressed envelopes provided by the bank. I have one account for each house and only one account per bank. This way all income and expenses for a particular house are in one checkbook. Each individual checkbook is kept in the property's file folder. Upon receipt of the rent and deposit slip the bank's mail teller credits the property's account immediately and sends me a notice of deposit with the time, date, amount, and the bank's name on it in the mail to my office. The check is well on its way to clearing We have proof in hand from a neutral third party that the rent was paid on time (to earn the rent discount), or not on time (tenant must pay rent in full plus any late charges to reinstate the right to the rent discount). When the deposit slip from the bank arrives at my office, I post it to the checkbook and pay the mortgages. My record keeping is over for the month unless there have been some operating expenses. Then I update my spread sheet (one sheet per house with 13 columns and 36 lines). Rents posted by month across line 1. At line 3 on down the page I list the various expenses and spread them by month. After subtracting the monthly expenses from the rent, the monthly net goes on line 36. At tax time my paperwork is just about complete.

Each house's income and expense totals and the net get transferred to a monthly summary sheet for an overall picture.

Use any system that is easy for you. Set the system up with the purchase of your first investment house. Don't do what I did and find yourself with seven apartment buildings, no record keeping system and three more buildings under purchase. That is not the time to decide you need a system. It took me months to get organized because I hadn't planned ahead. If you love computers, try keeping your records on it and let me know what happens.

NON-PAYMENT PROBLEMS: Every non-paying tenant would have loved to have paid me if he had the money. Once you have determined why the rent-money is lacking, it is decision time on your part. Every state has a procedure for eviction. Some are more effective than others. Some states seem to think a lease is a warranty deed. In the District of Columbia (where I have never been nor will ever be a landlord) by following the legal system rules, the eviction procedure can take as long as thirteen months if the tenant knows what he is doing. That's a l-o-n-g time without any rental income. Plus you get the thrill of watching the non-paying tenants slowly dismantle your building. Four or five of these disasters could wear down the toughest investor even with deep pockets. Be sure you seek competent legal advice <u>before</u> you need it. The costs of eviction can be brutal. Find out exactly what the legal costs are and add in the lost rent and your time and aggravation. Take a look at the grand total of all these costs and add in the potential destruction of the property by an irate tenant. Expensive is the word for it. There is a better way.

Review your non-paying tenants lease (any guarantors?). Then talk with the tenant in person. Stick to questions and listen to the answers. Never threaten anyone or you may have your bluff called. Win with sugar. 99% of the time they just don't have the money and would gladly move to a lesser and cheaper dwelling if they had some money for one month's security, one month's rent, and enough to cover moving expenses. Add these up in your head. If it's anything less than the cost of the eviction process, offer to put the money (cash) in escrow at your lawyer's office. The cash is his the day he is out (he's got three days), the place is cleaned to perfection (subject to your inspection and approval) and the keys are delivered to your lawyer.

REDUCING MANAGEMENT: There are a number of ways to lessen management and still retain a lot of the benefits of real estate. First, you can turn your portfolio of houses over to a qualified management company. I have never done this. Thus, I am not in a position to advise you. It would make common sense that no one cares about the ultimate well-being of an investment as much as the investor. Therefore, before entrusting your real estate to someone else, do a lot of research and digging about the experience and reputation of your potential manager. I would want to know how many houses he owns himself and how long he has had them.

In 1981, it occurred to me that if the tenants were also part owners of the property, they might tend to take better care and be more responsible about making timely payments. So, I set out to sell half of the ownership of my houses in the Raleigh area. A few existing tenants joined the plan. Most did not. Whenever I had a vacancy I placed ads in which I offered to rent the house, sell 100% of the house, or sell a 50% ownership position. From then on all the vacancies and newly acquired houses went into the program. In the years that followed I never had any problems whatsoever with my tenant/owners. A number of people have said there could be serious problems should the tenant/owner cease to make payments. So let caution be your guide. Once again, seek competent legal help. Here's my equity sharing program.

I met with people who responded to my ads to explain the three alternatives: rent, buy or share ownership. Once they understood the benefits of the latter, almost all went for the deal. Since I took title to the S/F houses in trust, it was easy to set up a contract for the new tenant/owners to purchase their share over a period of time. Their monthly payments became one half mortgage payment and one half rent. They assigned their contract for their one half beneficial interest as security for their lease to me. A default on the lease voided their contract. They made their monthly payments to the designated record account set up in a local bank. This would establish a clear record as to the timeliness of their payments. The bank, for a small service charge, made the necessary monthly mortgage payments. I took my net monthly profit out by writing a check on the account. For tax purposes we split the deductible expenses.

Everyone was happy. The tenant/owners were buying into a home which they could not afford otherwise. They got more tax benefits than they would have by renting. They were highly motivated to maintain and repair their home and were motivated to make their monthly payment early because part of each payment was building equity that benefitted them. They knew that if they ever had financial problems, they could notify me that they would be paying their monthly payments with their built up equity in their contract for the beneficial interest.

The term of my agreement with the tenant/owners was into perpetuity. There was no required buy-out at anytime by either side. If they wanted to sell the property, I was the first buyer they called. Our agreement called for five opinions of value by five Realtors® chosen by the tenant/owners. We arranged opinions-of-value in descending order and discarded the highest and the lowest values. The middle three estimates of value were averaged and that number became the "fair market value" of the property. Their share depended upon how much equity they had build up or used up in their contract for one half of the beneficial interest. My agreement was to buy them out with cash or, at their option, I would repeat the whole process in their new home.

I was happy because I had a very passive investment which allowed for twice as many houses with motivated tenant/owners. Also my average cash flow per house was over $100 a month more than if I had rented outright. And I was able to do all these transactions without putting up any money.

Remember, there can be problems with equity participation deals. Structure them carefully and, as always, be completely above board in a manner that all parties fully understand what is going on.

SHARED OWNERSHIP CONTINUED: A friend of mine owns over 50% of thirty houses without any management headaches. He gets an annual statement and one net check per year per house from different manager/co-owners. Whenever he finds a "good" deal he puts the transaction together and structures in enough room to include his favorite local manager. When all is signed, sealed and delivered, he is off to another deal. This might be a goal worthy of pursuing.

Another sharp idea is to sell at deep discount (with an option back, say, for ten years) one or more of your investment houses to a trusted friend who owns a large number of houses and is an expert manager. As long as you have a recorded "notice of contract" against the property, your position is secure and you can go on to other deals for ten years only to buy back into the property at an agreed upon strike price. There are dozens of way to structure this transaction depending on your needs and those of your trusted friend.

Whatever your real estate management needs, always strive to learn more and better techniques. There are a lot of experienced seminar teachers willing to share their secrets with you. Your attitudes toward hands on management might change with time and it would be nice to have some alternatives.

"Have you hugged your tenant today?"

REAL ESTATE DIVESTITURE

REAL ESTATE DIVESTITURE

If the object of the game is the acquisition of properties, then why consider divestiture? "Why would I sell what I have worked so hard to acquire?" An excellent question with numerous answers.

Each January in Pascagoula, Mississippi, "Smokey" Joe West sits down in his office to do his annual "culling." I first learned of this practice when I called Smokey one January years ago. In his soft southern drawl, he explained that he was evaluating each and every single family he had in his portfolio. With 50 to 60 houses this could be a job. I was curious as to how he was ranking them. "Let's look at one house as an example," he said. "I do the mathematics based upon how much I originally put into it and how much it has cost me over the holding period and how much cash flow it has thrown off to date. If the numbers look great, it's a keeper. If the numbers are a bit shaky, I put it in the 'review' pile. If the numbers are poor, the file gets put on the 'to go' pile. When I'm done with the math part, I go back over the review pile one more time evaluate it in regards to the amount of management it has required. If it hasn't taken any of my time I'll keep it. If the property or the tenants have been a real pain, it goes." In his outward appearance, Smokey is soft spoken, kind and you might think him a bit slow. Wrong!!! His brain is moving at a mile a minute and it never stops. He is a great friend and has helped me more than he knows.

Practice culling your portfolio and soon you'll understand the need for divestiture. The most serious aspect of selling might well be the tax implications. Do your tax mathematics with your CPA long before you put up the for sale sign. Once you understand the tax ramifications of an all-cash sale, you might want to do a few trial runs using owner financing, 1031 exchanging, trade with a buy-back provision or any of hundreds of ways to lessen the tax impact. Is it property held for investment or does it fit the dealer rules of the tax code? Do some serious thinking as to why you are motivated or need to sell. Defining your needs beforehand will help you expand the market of takers for your property. The more flexible and open-minded your thinking is, the sooner you will be out of title.

An all-cash sale might seem ideal, but after review with your CPA it appears the government will get more than you care to part with.

Let's consider a few other ways to go out of title. Make a gift to a qualified charitable institution and receive an annuity for life. (Not something I have ever done, but I understand the mechanics). Consider establishing a trust for the benefit of your children and grand children and funding the trust with the property. Consider selling a one-half interest to your present tenant. Get together with a group of friends who also invest in houses in the area. Have everyone contribute one house to a trust and turn the management of all the houses over to a qualified management company with the idea that you will divest everything in eight years and split the proceeds. With a little thought and "idea tracking" you will come up with dozens of things to do with the ownership of the property.

1031 EXCHANGES: "No gain or loss is recognized upon the exchange of property held for productive use in a trade or business or for investment, solely for property of like kind to be held either for productive use in a business or for investment." (Code Sec. 1031) You would be well advised to read the entire 1031 code section as well as the case law pertaining to the section's rules and uses. There are numerous seminars and books on the subject. Attend one or two if you are uncertain about how it works. A thorough discussion here is beyond the scope of this manual.

However, an important tool I use all the time is most helpful in balancing the equities in any exchange. The tool is called the "T" Bar. It is simple to construct and easy to remember. Take a blank piece of paper and draw a line across the page about two inches from the top. Then split the page in half with a vertical line drawn top to bottom. Now you have you "T" Bar. On the left side write the following terms:

OWNER'S VALUE
EXISTING DEBT
EQUITY:
BOOT:
BALANCE:

That's the form. Let's take a real world example so we can see the form work for us. You have a S/F house with an existing mortgage balance of $26,000 and an Owner's Value of $78,000. You offer to exchange your S/F house for my commercial land worth $130,000 with a debt of $60,000 (and a land lease in place for $900/month—enough to cover the PITI and the tenant has a contract to purchase in three years at $150,000). Let's balance the transaction on the following "T" Bar.

	S/F HOUSE	COMMERCIAL LAND
OWNER'S VALUE:	$78,000	$130,000
DEBT:	$26,000	$ 60,000
EQUITY:	$52,000	$ 70,000
BOOT:	$18,000	- 0 -
BALANCE:	$70,000	$ 70,000

The key to balancing exchanges is understanding and using the "T" Bar. First draw and label one. Next fill in the givens (the Existing Debt and the Owner's Value) on both sides. Then subtract the debt from the Owner's Value to determine the Equity line on both properties.

Whichever equity is bigger, put "-0-" on the Boot line and bring the equity number to the bottom line ("Balance"). Whatever that balance number is (in this case $70,000) put it in "Balance" in the other column (in this case under the S/F house column).

One last step. At this point the only box left open is the one in the single family column beside the word "BOOT." Subtract the Equity amount ($52,000 in our example) from the Balance amount ($70,000) and the answer for the Boot box in the S/F house column equals $18,000.

This means that you must add $18,0000 worth of something for us to have a deal. It could be cash, paper or any number of things. You are now able to balance any size transaction with any number of legs. The "T" Bar has been a wonderful and profit making tool for me.

PAPER AS A DIVESTING TOOL: Real estate secured Paper is the topic of the entire second half of this manual. There you will gain a working knowledge of Paper or add to the one you already have. Almost all the paper I have ever bought was created to sell the real estate—not to create the Paper. There are a number of ways to structure Paper to your future advantage when you decide to sell your real estate and hold the financing for the buyer. Here a few ideas.

Assume, for the sake of example, you have sold a free and clear S/F house with $30,000 down and have agreed to carry back an $80,000 first for 30 years at 10% with no balloon. Most people carry a first deed of trust and that's that. Until they need some cash down the road. When they go to sell the Paper, they are shocked at how big the discount is. Try this.

Determine what the monthly would be on the entire loan ($702.06). Then create a new first and second deed of trust with two separate notes. Make the first note and mortgage for $30,000 at the same rate of 10% and assign it 100% of the total monthly payments ($702.06). How soon will it amortize out? (53 months). What is the Loan Constant? (28%).

By allocating all of the payment to the $30,000 first mortgage, should you ever need to raise cash in a hurry, you will get something close to par and still have the right to collect the $702.06 per month starting with the 54th month for another 307 months.

Another idea along this line is to create one $80,000 first mortgage with the same monthly payment as above ($702.06) and eight $10,000 notes secured by the same first mortgage. The payment per note would be $70.20. The new owner would make payments to a trustee. All of the monies on the eight notes would be yours until you sold one or traded one for a car or a boat or a three month vacation to New Zealand. Then the trustee would be instructed to make one of the $70.20 monthly payments to whomever you had traded the note. This is just another method of making change out of Paper by planning ahead.

AVOIDING DISCOUNT IF YOU NEED TO CASH OUT YOUR PAPER: Most Paper holders needing to cash out of their Paper wind up taking a substantial discount when they sell for cash. To lessen the discount impact, trade your paper, say a $15,000 well-secured note, to someone who could use the income stream rather than their $15,000 car. Once you have title to the car sell the car for cash. With one extra step you have gone from Paper to cash with little or no discount.

BORROWING WITH REAL ESTATE: Sometimes people feel divestiture of real estate is the only way to raise cash for other investments, but they really don't want to sell the property. There is a way around this without going to commercial lenders. I discovered this formula quite by accident in a transaction I was doing to raise money in order to buy more real estate secured paper and have since used it many times for many different reasons. Here is the Borrowing With Real Estate Formula.

Suppose you own a free and clear S/F house valued at $80,000 which you would like to keep and you knew about a great deal where you could get a $95,000 house for $50,000 cash only. You write a contract on the property for $50,000 cash to close in 90 days. Now, where to get the money? Banks are out because of your aversion to giving out your social security number.

Step One: you look around in your local market place and locate a $60,000 house for sale. The seller, Mrs. York, will carry all paper at 8% direct reduction for 20 years provided she has ample security. You offer Mrs. York a $60,000 note at 8% for 240 months with payments of $501.86 SECURED BY THE S/F HOUSE YOU PRESENTLY OWN AND WHICH YOU DO NOT WISH TO SELL AND WOULD LIKE TO KEEP FOR A LONG TIME. By using your investment house worth $80,000 as security of the $60,000 note and first mortgage owed to Mrs. York, she delivers her house to you free and clear and promptly moves to Florida.

Step Two: You call a rehab friend of yours who will pay $50,000 cash and not a dime more for the house you have just bought from Mrs. York for $60,000. Fine, you take his $50,000 in cash and give him the deed to your $60,000 house.

You take your $50,000 cash from your sale to the rehabber and close on the $95,000 house you are buying for $50,000 cash. Done.

Read the above example one more time. What you have done is borrowed $50,000 cash costing $501.86 for 240 months payable to Mrs. York. Your cost of your money is 10.58% interest rate per year. And by investing the $50,000 cash into a great deal ($95,000 house for $50,000 is not too bad and the house is free and clear), you are able to clean up and rent the place for $875 per month which covers the taxes and insurance as well as the $501.86 you pay to Mrs. York. You started with an $80,000 equity (which now has $20,000 equity) plus a free and clear $95,000 equity in your new house. You have increased your equity position by $35,000 and your monthly cash flow by over

$150.00 and you have a $10,000 ordinary loss against income for tax purposes. I just tell people I must not be too bright—how many people do you know who can buy something for $60,000 and sell it the same day for $50,000 and make a profit?

I hope you are getting the sense that the number of ways to acquire, hold and divest real estate are immense and very often real estate transactions become entwined with Paper secured by real estate To go far in real estate you have to fully understand Paper. In the next section we'll take a good look at Paper.

PAPER ACQUISITION

PAPER ACQUISITION

Why acquire Paper?

Because Paper is a source of cash flows and profits through discount earned. It is a predictable and determinable income stream. The Paper market is huge and all around us. Basically there is an unlimited supply with more being created daily around the world. Paper backed by real estate (and properly purchased) can be a very secure investment. The investment yields are easy to calculate. Paper is very low management when the payments are on time. There are lots of creative things that can be done with paper—not only when it is created, but also while it is being held and when it is sold.

That's the good news.

The bad news is Paper can be a real fire drill if the payor should default. Unless you do your homework thoroughly, paper is complicated enough to bite you. You must be absolutely certain you are getting 100% of what you paid for. Unlike real estate ownership there are no tax benefits from owning paper. Like any other investment, the investor needs to be extremely careful. Remember, if it seems too good to be true it's not.

IMPORTANT PAPER CONCEPTS: In order to bring all of my readers up to speed, let me discuss briefly the essential basics of Paper.

The definition of Paper is "Any document that records a promise of payment sometime in the future." Examples of Paper would be I.O.U.s, stocks, bonds, certificates of deposit, social security, pension plans, I.R.A.s, Keoghs, leases, Treasury notes, Treasury bonds, accounts receivable, timber rights, mineral rights, tobacco allotments, deeds, options, mortgages and deeds of trust, to name a few. My favorite is and has been Mortgages and Deeds of Trust.

Next, as you can see from the above list, Paper is an income stream generator. Another way of putting it would be to call them "annuities."

Annuities (income streams), each and every one of them, have TWO critical items: "Ns" (number of payments and payment spacing) and "PMTs" (the dollar amount of each promised payment). So far so good.

Next, the concept of "present value." It is simple. "A dollar in the future is worth less than a dollar today." Therefore, when we purchase the right to receive a payment or a number of payments we should always pay something less than the amount promised. Sounds like "discounting." It is, which is the next topic.

"Discounting" is the mathematical process of reducing all future payments down to today's (present) value in order to reflect the impact time has on money. The greater the time span until we receive the money, the less it is worth today.

"All of this is nice. So what?"

Well, if Paper is a promise of "Ns" and "PMTs" sometime in the future, wouldn't it be great if there were a way to discount all those future payments to today's dollars and at the same time show us the yield (return) on our monies invested? There is a way.

Financial calculators have been around twenty-five years, and hopefully you have one that you can operate. Once you understand that

Paper is just a series of Ns and PMTs (look for these symbols on your financial calculator) you can easily determine how much to pay to achieved a specified yield. Or you can calculate the yield if you know the price asked for an income stream (Ns and PMTs).

That's it, friends. That is as succinctly as I've ever put it. The following case will get you started punching the keys of your financial calculator.

SITUATION:

PROBLEM:

POTENTIAL SOLUTION:

CASE: ANALYZING A PAPER INCOME STREAM

A $10,000 note is offered to you for sale for $5,800 and the seller is desperate (pressure from the IRS). The face interest is 8% and the payments are $121.33 per month. 90 remain of the original 120 months. Your company's pension fund will not let you invest in paper below a 13% yield. What is the investment yield of the above situation?

What are you buying for $5,800? The right to receive 90 monthly payments of $121.33. Get your financial calculator and put the "givens" information in the proper keys:

90 keyed into N (number of payments). You are buying 90 of payments.

121.33 keyed into PMT (the amount of each payment) You will be receiving $121.33 each month.

-5,800 keyed into PV (the amount you are spending today for the right to receive the income stream) **Notice the negative sign** before the 5,800. You are spending the money so it is expressed as negative. SOLVE FOR I (your yield will flash up expressed in the monthly yield rate. Just multiply the I number by 12 (the payments are expressed in months) and you will see your yield is 18.9%. OK for the pension fund to purchase if everything else checks out.

BUYING EXISTING PAPER VERSUS MAKING LOANS: The following is a list of the pros and cons of lending money versus buying existing Paper at a discount. When you have finished the list, you will understand why I like discounted Paper rather than hard money loans.

FACTORS	LOANS	DISCOUNT
Track Record	No	Yes
Equity Build-up	No	Yes
Property Appreciation	No	Probably
Low Interest Rates	Market	Yes
High Yields	Market	Higher
Cash Invested	105%	40% - 70%
Availability of Paper	Yes	Less
Profitability	Mostly	Yes
Usury Laws	Yes	No
Guarantor Parties	One	Two
Properties Securing Note	One	Often Two
Payors Used to Making Payments	Not yet	Yes
My Experience to Date	Problems	No Problem

NEGOTIABLE PROMISSORY NOTE: According to the Uniform Commercial Code (UCC) there are certain minimum conditions that must be present for a debt instrument to be classified as a "negotiable instrument." These are the only type I have ever dealt with and probably the only type you would consider purchasing. Here are the requirements.

To be negotiable, a promissory note: MUST BE IN WRITING, STATE A DATE OF ISSUE, STATE THE OBLIGATION AMOUNT, NAME A PAYEE OR BEARER OR CASH, HAVE A DUE DATE OR BE ON DEMAND, PROMISE TO PAY UNCONDITIONALLY, AND, HAVE THE MAKER'S SIGNATURE.

If you should ever need to recall these seven items, just look at a blank check. Obviously its worthless until written upon, there's a place for the date; "pay to the order of" is an unconditional promise to pay; beside which is the line for the Payee's name, bearer, or cash; then a line for the amount payable; a check is almost always "on demand"; and there is the line for the maker's signature. Now you've got and you won't forget the legal definition of "Negotiable Promissory Note." Most, but not all, negotiable instruments contain additional terms pertaining to how the debt will be repaid such as interest (rent for the use of money); location to which the payment is to be sent; partial payments either monthly, quarterly, biennial, annual; as well as terms and conditions defining default and methods of correcting default. Also penalties for late payment and default.

Legal fees for collection are almost always the cost of the maker and will be stated in the instrument.

SECURITY FOR THE DEBT: There are six areas to discuss concerning "security for the debt" in the field of real-estate-secured Paper. They are as follows: 1. The Property 2. The Documents 3. The Track record 4. The Payor 5. The Seller of the note 6. Legal Counsel.

THE PROPERTY: When you are considering buying a note secured by real estate - STOP - Look at every aspect of the physical property pledged as security. Look at it as though you were buying the real estate, lock, stock and barrel. Because if the note goes into default and you must foreclose, you WILL have bought the property. Until the note is paid off in full, you just about do own the property.

THE DOCUMENTS: This is the place most of us get in trouble in buying Paper. Good legal help here can make all the difference until you are your own best expert. First, there is the note. Read and reread it to see if it conforms to the UCC rules of negotiable promissory notes. The tighter the wording and the better it anticipates problems the more valuable it becomes. Second, the deeds of trust (or mortgage) must be read and understood completely. There can be no glitches here or the problems can come back to haunt you. Make sure that all the necessary instruments have been recorded and that there is a title policy in place. Read the title policy. Learn to run your own titles in the local registry of deeds. I always do.

I know of a case where a lawyer sold a note and "second" deed of trust in Maryland to an investor who later became my client. The paperwork was all his and now my client was no longer receiving the payments. After doing all my homework which revealed a great deal, we went to see him at his office and I asked "Counselor, what do you plan to do?" Those were the only words I spoke. He promptly wrote a check for all the back interest and principal and fees. He announced he would institute foreclosure immediately in his name. We departed, cashed the check and mailed all the necessary paper work back to him. And now for the rest of the story.

My homework had uncovered the following facts: the first mortgagee was in the final stages of foreclosure which was just a few days off. Secondly, even thought the attorney had written and received a title policy, his deed of trust had never been recorded in the registry of deeds. My client had been kept whole and the attorney was out over $50,000 with no chance of recovery. Do your homework completely before you hand over the money.

After you and your legal counsel have determined that the note instrument conforms to the UCC rules, your state's laws, and is tough enough to cover all contingencies, take a hard look at the deed of trust (or mortgage). This is the document which pledges a real estate asset to the creditor until the obligation has been paid in full. It must be tough, straightforward and powerful enough to anticipate any and all potential problems. Make sure your copy has the Book and Page or its recordation in the county registry of deeds. Read and reread it a number of times with a highlighter and a red pencil in hand making certain that all the essentials are there. Look for references to other recorded instruments which might lessen or increase the effect of the deed of trust. 8e sure to understand the impact of any easements described in the legal description. A good practice exercise is to go to the registry of deeds, run a few titles and make copies of all the different mortgages you can find such as banks, hard money lenders, purchase money mortgages, etc. Study them until they make sense to you. What you do not understand, seek legal counsel for an explanation. This will be very educational and time well spent.

THE SETTLEMENT SHEET AND ALL OTHER DOCUMENTS: The seller of a note should have all these instruments in his files from the closing when the note was created. Get copies, review them all in detail and be certain the paperwork makes logical sense. If it doesn't, get the necessary answers. Otherwise move on to another deal.

THE TRACK RECORD: An important part of the security is the payment history. The record of payments, timely or otherwise is a fair indication of what will happen in the future (perhaps). A poor track record is not necessarily a reason abandon your efforts to purchase the Paper. Attempt to find out why the payments have been erratic or late. There may be a real estate opportunity here as well as a paper profit. However, do not buy "problem" paper unless you know the solution to the problem.

THE PAYOR OF THE NOTE: Garner as much information and background as is possible concerning the payor. Does he live in the property?

Where does he work? What is his profession or skills and is he concerned about his reputation in the community? Is he a hands-on type owner who works full-time on his numerous properties? There are lots of questions which will give you a better understanding of the payor. My concern with the profile of the payor has never been as great as my concern for the equity in the property and the note for sale because in times of trouble you may ultimately have to look to the property to protect your investment. As a footnote, sometimes you will find the note has been guaranteed by another party. You would want to find out who they are and what relationship they have with the payor. This can only add to the payee's security.

THE SELLER OF THE NOTE: In the purchasing negotiations you should make it your goal to learn everything possible about the seller of the Paper. This knowledge will be very helpful in a number of ways. It will help you create your best offer by matching your benefits to his needs. Also, you will want him to guarantee (sell "with recourse") the payments. By having the seller assign the note with recourse you will pick up additional security should you need it in the future. Sometimes the other security is so strong that I do not push the issue. Use your judgment in each case.

LEGAL COUNSEL: Here is your last and often best source of security. When I started buying Paper many years ago, I made it the rule to review the documents of the deal with my lawyer. This is essential, for it educated me to the rules and laws of the game. The review made certain that everything was in order and would withstand assault from any quarter. I always had my lawyer close the transaction in his office. After attending a few settlements I found it unnecessary to be there. Rather, upon reviewing the deal with him, I would put the purchase amount in his escrow account and pay him for his legal advice by separate check. He was perfectly capable of settlement without me. Finally, because I had paid him for the correctness of all the documents and his legal counsel, I knew he was bound to correct and defend any problem with the paperwork down the road. This was just one more ounce of protection for my investment.

NEGOTIATING FOR PAPER: The art of negotiating applies to Paper, just as it does to real estate or anything else you might set out to purchase. The rules are the same:

1. Stick to kind, understanding, and information-gathering type questions.
2. Probe to fully understand what the seller's situation is.
3. Learn to listen to the answers with your "inner" ear (gut feeling)as well as your ears.
4. After much questioning and listening, the "real" problem (needs)and the motivation will begin to appear.
5. There are as many "potential solutions" as there are needs. This is where your experience and creativity come into play. Offer no more than absolutely necessary to fulfill the needs.
6. Learn to describe the benefits of your offer in terms of the Seller's needs.

SOME FINER POINTS ON THE ART OF NEGOTIATING:

* He who mentions price or terms first loses.
* Find out what else the seller can add to the transaction.
* Determine if the seller doesn't need all the cash now.
* Always ask questions. Never use a declarative sentence.
* When someone answers "no" ask "why not?"
* People are much more motivated to respond with "no" than "yes" so make "no" mean "yes" by posing your question: "Is there any reason why we couldn't consider...?" when he answers "No" move on to your proposal.
* Study body language all the time. It will tell you what is going on in the subconscious mind.
* Once you have asked a question, wait for the answer. Never fear silence no matter how long it takes for the answer to come back.
* If you are talking, you are not learning.
* If you must talk, choose your words carefully.
* Make promises slowly and very thoughtfully. Promises are the foundation of your reputation.

* Practice the art of negotiating at home with your children. These counseling techniques can eliminate all need for anger.
* Never burn your bridges.
* He who becomes angry is out of control and always loses.
* If the deal suits your needs, get a contract (subject to verification of the information) or an option for a period of time long enough to verify every detail.
* If the deal does not suit your needs, always try to get an option. This will give you time to rethink your position and to see if someone else might like the opportunity.

The following check list will give you some more ideas of the important information you will need:

A CHECK LIST FOR PAPER

1. The Note
2. The Mortgage, Deed of Trust or other security instrument
3. The Settlement Sheet created at the time of note creation
4. The Payment Records
5. The Amortization Schedule (You might check to see if the payment amount is correct.)
6. Annual Property Operating information
7. A copy of everything that is recorded against the property
8. A title run on the Seller to see if there are any judgments or liens against the note he is trying to sell.
9. Estoppel letters from the Payor and any senior lien holders
10. Copies of any senior notes
11. Real estate tax bills, past and present
12. Any indication of partial sales of the real estate by the payor
13. Photos of the property—take your own if you need to List of all improvements to the property

14. List of all improvements to the property
15. Copy of the listing agreement when the property was sold
16. Copies of surveys, timber cruise, and any other professional studies
17. Copies of leases presently in force
18. List of partial sales of the paper you are trying to buy
19. Addresses of the Property, Note holders, Mortgage broker, Payors, settlement attorneys, title company and phone numbers where applicable.
20. Corporate resolutions to sell the paper if seller is incorporated
21. All appraisals and a list of comparable sales
22. Title report and title policy
23. Fire/liability insurance policy naming the holder of the note as insured
24. Guarantee contracts of the note, if any
25. Names, addresses, and phone numbers of any and all advisers the seller relies upon
26. Anything else pertaining to the Note, the Property, the Payor, the Payee, the Situation, the Problem or the Potential Solution

THE PAPER ACQUISITION FOLDER:

In my years of lecturing and teaching about Paper, I found that a student would return home after the seminar and be at a loss as to what to do next. To overcome this problem I created a dozen essential pages which fit into a letter-size manila folder that could be reproduced and carried to each meeting with a prospective Paper seller. AFTER REVIEWING THE INFORMATION WITH YOUR LEGAL COUNSEL, feel free to improve it and to use it. It is called: "The Paper Acquisition Folder."

Editor's Note: For a downloadable version of The Paper Acquisition Folder go to

http://therealestateinvestingzone.com/paper-acquisition-folder/

and enter the password: papert

THE PAPER ACQUISITION FOLDER

PAPER INFORMATION SHEET

DATE:

HOLDER(S):

ADDRESS:

PHONE:

SOURCE:

NOTE FOR SALE: ORIGINAL NOW

(1st mortgage)

BALANCE: (PV)

INTEREST: (I)

PMT/MO: (PMT)

TERM: (N)

BALLOONS: (FV)

LOAN CONSTANT:

CREATION DATE:

OF PMTs LEFT:

WHY SELLING?:

SELLER'S NEEDS: $__________ (YTM) ____%

HOW SOON?:______________

PROPERTY

ADDRESS:

PROP. TYPE: AGE:

ASSESSOR'S INFO:

ASSESSMENT: TAXES:

CONDITION:

SALE PRICE: $ DOWN PAYMENT: $

LTV RATIO: % PAYOR OCCUPIED?:

DOCUMENTS FROM NOTE SELLER (COPIES)

NOTE	MORTGAGE/DEED OF TRUST
APPRAISAL REPORT	TITLE POLICY AND REPORT
ALL SENIOR LIENS	SETTLEMENT SHEET
DEED	INSURANCE POLICIES

NEXT APPOINTMENT WITH SELLERS: ________________

OFFERED FOR PURCHASE $________________
(OR NEXT STEP IN PURCHASING)

AGREED UPON CONTRACT
PURCHASE PRICE $________________

SETTLEMENT DATE: ______________________

TITLE COMPANY: ______________________

SETTLEMENT LOCATION: ________________

PHONE NUMBERS: ______________________

EMAIL ADDRESSES: ____________________

A CHECK LIST FOR PAPER

1. The Note
2. The Mortgage, Deed of Trust or other security instrument
3. The Settlement Sheet created at the time of note creation
4. The Payment Records
5. The Amortization Schedule (You might check to see if the payment amount is correct.)
6. Annual Property Operating information
7. A copy of everything that is recorded against the property
8. A title run on the Seller to see if there are any judgments or liens against the note he is trying to sell.
9. Estoppel letters from the Payor and any senior lien holders
10. Copies of any senior notes
11. Real estate tax bills, past and present
12. Any indication of partial sales of the real estate by the payor
13. Photos of the property—take your own if you need to List of all improvements to the property

14. List of all improvements to the property
15. Copy of the listing agreement when the property was sold
16. Copies of surveys, timber cruise, and any other professional studies
17. Copies of leases presently in force
18. List of partial sales of the paper you are trying to buy
19. Addresses of the Property, Note holders, Mortgage broker, Payors, settlement attorneys, title company and phone numbers where applicable.
20. Corporate resolutions to sell the paper if seller is incorporated
21. All appraisals and a list of comparable sales
22. Title report and title policy
23. Fire/liability insurance policy naming the holder of the note as insured
24. Guarantee contracts of the note, if any
25. Names, addresses, and phone numbers of any and all advisers the seller relies upon
26. Anything else pertaining to the Note, the Property, the Payor, the Payee, the Situation, the Problem or the Potential Solution

PROPERTY DESCRIPTION

NEIGHBORHOOD:

LOT/LAND:

DWELLING:

INTERIOR

EXTERIOR

OTHER BUILDINGS:

POOL?:

GENERAL OVERALL IMPRESSION:

ADDITIONAL PAPERWORK NEEDED TODAY

ORIGINAL SETTLEMENT SHEET (Need Copies)

SENIOR LOAN INFORMATION (Need Copies)

APPRAISAL INFORMATION (Need copies)

TITLE POLICY INFORMATION (Need Copies)

PROPERTY INSURANCE (Need copies)

PAYMENT RECORDS AND HISTORY

PAYMENT RECORD (Need copy of amortization schedule)

AMOUNT DUE: $

FREQUENCY:

FIRST PAYMENT DATE:

WHEN DUE:

LATE CHARGES: $

HOW OFTEN:

IN ARREARS NOW?:

PAYMENTS SENT TO:

ADDITIONAL INFORMATION:

OFFER TO ASSIGN AND TO SELL A NOTE AND DEED OF TRUST

FOR VALUABLE CONSIDERATION, I (we), the undersigned ____________________________(SELLER), offer and agree to assign, to convey and sell to_______________________________________ (BUYER), his successors or assigns, the note and deed of trust held by the undersigned on which the PAYOR is: (Name, address and phone of Payor)____

____

____

For ________________________ DOLLARS to be paid as follows:

(Terms and schedule of purchase payment)

The said deed of trust is recorded in ____________________ County, State of _________________, in the Registry of Deeds, BOOK _______ PAGE _______

and dated _______________________.

Property address is

____

____

The approximate principal balance as of _________________________ on the said note and deed of trust is $____________ and the monthly payment is $_____________ per month. There are ______ payments remaining. The next payment is due on ____________________.

The PAYOR has ____ been late in making payments and the payments are now ________ months in arrears.

I (we) fully warrant that I have disclosed all information of which a prudent purchaser should be aware.

The BUYER, his successors or assigns shall have until ________________ to exercise and accept this offer to assign and sell. Acceptance shall be by written notice to the seller, with the settlement to be held on or before __________________ at _________________

____

At settlement, seller will provide, in addition to the ORIGINAL NOTE and the ORIGINAL DEED OF TRUST, the following:

Seller is advised that this is a binding contract to assign and to sell the above described note and deed of trust and if it is not fully understood, legal counsel should be consulting before signing.

Dated: , 19

____________________ ____________________

ASSIGNOR ASSIGNOR

OPTION TO PURCHASE REAL ESTATE SECURED NOTE AND DEED OF TRUST

Option is granted this _____ day of _____________, 19____ , by ___________________ (OPTIONOR)

To (OPTIONEE)

for valuable consideration granted by the Optionee to the Optionor, the receipt of which is hereby acknowledged, and by this option, the Optionor hereby grants to the holder in due course the exclusive right for and during the period of ninety (90) days from the date hereof, to purchase the below described note(s) and security instruments presently owned by the Optionor, for the amount of $

The said note(s) and security instruments are described as follows:

These payments and obligations are secured by Real Estate located and described as follow:

The Optionor hereby warrants that the attached Exhibits are in fact photocopies and reflect a true statement of condition of the debt instruments, of the security instruments, of the payments, of the Payors, and of balances currently owed to the Optionor, is bound by this contract not to dispose of, nor to pledge, nor to assign, and not to alter in any manner the above described documents during the period of this option contract.

Date:

__________________________ __________________________

OPTIONOR OPTIONOR

____

Street address

____

City State Zip Telephone

ESTOPPEL LETTER TO THE PAYOR

Note Purchaser, Inc.
P.O. Box 1000
Manitou Springs, CO 12345

March 14th 1991

Mr. and Mrs Happy Payor
456 That Street
Nowhere, Virginia

Dear Mr. and Mrs. Payor:

It has become necessary for this company to verify certain information pertaining to the accounts of Mr. and Mrs. George Payee. At the time of purchase on December 21st, 1989 you signed a note and deed of trust in favor of Mr. and Mrs. Payee in the original balance of $15,000 and the outstanding balance now being $14,492.16.

It is our understanding that you have made to date 27 monthly payments of $198.23 to amortize the debt. Hopefully our numbers are in agreement. Would you please verify the above information as correct by signing on the line at the bottom of this letter . Enclosed please find a return addressed stamped envelope for you convenience.

Thank you in advance for you help and cooperation.

Sincerely,

P. Thorpe, President

Acknowledged by Mr. and Mrs. Happy Payor

To the Reader of this manual: Traditionally Payors will not return your request for verification (estoppel). They throw the letter away. So years ago I took a different tack. Notice in the above letter where I mention the existing outstanding balance. The amount stated is $14,492.16. The correct amount owed by them is $12,793.06. I always get a letter setting me straight by return mail. So much for the problem of Payors not responding to estoppel letters.

LETTER TO INSURER

Mr. and Mrs. Note Seller
9876 First street
Big City, Iowa

April 1, 1991

XYZ Insurance Company
123 Jump Street
Anytown, VA

RE: Policy Number: Policy Name: Property Owner: Property Address

Dear Sirs:
You are hereby notified that an interest in a deed of trust secured by the above property has been purchased by ________________________.

Please add the below named as beneficiary to the above described policy as Loss Payee.

Should there be a lapse of insurance due to a non-payment of the premium, please notify the note purchaser at the address below.

Sincerely,

(Seller of the Note)

Information about the Purchaser (new beneficiary)

Name
Mailing Address
Telephone

PAYMENT INSTRUCTION LETTER TO THE PAYOR

Note Purchaser Inc.
P.O. Box 1000
Manitou Springs, CO 12345

April 1, 1991

Mr. and Mrs. Happy Payor
456 That Street
Nowhere, Virginia

Dear Mr. and Mrs. Payor:

On this date the note and deed of trust made payable to Mr. and Mrs. George Payee, secured by your property located at

____

has been assigned to the Note Purchaser, Inc. This assignment does not affect in any manner the original terms and conditions of your note and deed of trust.

Beginning with your next payment, due April 21st, you are requested to mail all future payments due on the 21st of each month to:

Note Purchaser, Inc.
P.O. Box 1000
Manitou Springs, Co 12345
Please make checks payable to Note Purchaser, Inc.

The present balance on the note and deed of trust is $12,793.06, the monthly payments being $198.23 per month. Should there be any questions or problems at any time, do not hesitate to contact this office.

Sincerely,

P. Thorpe, President

Acknowledged by Mr. and Mrs. George Payee

ASSIGNMENT OF DEED OF TRUST

For valuable consideration in hand paid, receipt where of is hereby acknowledged, ____ hereby set over, transfer, and assign unto ____, heirs, executors, administrators or assigns all of its rights, title and interest in and to ____, that certain deed of trust, together with note it was given to secure, executed by ____, to (Trustee for) __________________________, in the stated amount of $_______________, dated the _____ day of _____________ ,19__ and duly recorded in the office of the Registrar of Deeds (or the Clerk of Court), for the County of _____________________________, State of _________________, in BOOK _______ PAGE _______

THE LEGAL DESCRIPTION FOR SAID PROPERTY BEING

Witness hand and deal this _____ day of_________, 19_____

Witness By:

(SEAL)

Witness By:

(SEAL)

STATE OF
COUNTY OF

I, ____, a NOTARY PUBLIC in and for the ____, DO HEREBY CERTIFY THAT
party to a certain Assignment bearing the date of __________________________
and hereto annexed, personally appeared before me in said _______. THE SAID ________________
being personally known by me as the person who executed the said Assignment and acknowledged the same to be their free act and deed given under my hand and seal this _____day of __________, 19___

My commission expires

Notary Public

THIS DOCUMENT PREPARED BY:

SETTLEMENT CHECK LIST

SETTLEMENT:

Time:

Date:

Location:

Agent:

Phone:

Notification of sellers of all of the above:

BRING TO SETTLEMENT:

Completed file folder

Bank check for seller of note made payable to buyer (to be endorsed over to seller at end of settlement)

Checkbook

Letter of insurance notification

Letter to payor

TO BE DONE AT SETTLEMENT:

Note endorsed

Assignment signed, witnessed and notarized

Letters signed

Take possession of:

- Original note
- Original deed of trust
- Original title policy pay
- Any fees due
- Endorse purchase check over to payee
- Make copies of everything

Names, addresses and phone numbers of everyone present:

POST-SETTLEMENT SCHEDULE:

Record necessary documents at registry of deeds

Place original note and deed of trust in safe deposit box

Enter location of originals in "location-of-originals" log

Set up new payee account on master records

Mail:

Letter to insurance company

Letter to payor

Letter and complete package to my investor (if there is one)

NEGOTIATING HINTS

Key 1: Stick to questions.

Key 2: Listen to the answers.

Key 3: Try to fully understand the situation.

Key 4: Be friendly; but really listen.

Key 5: Try to determine what the problem really is.

Key 6: Why are they really selling their paper?

Key 7: Do not think about potential solutions until you are certain you and they understand their problem.

Key 8: How much and how soon do they need the money?

Key 9: Remember: talk about your benefits in terms of their needs.

Key 10: Keep your financial calculator out of sight.

SOME POTENTIAL SOLUTIONS
(THINK OF AS MANY POTENTIAL SOLUTIONS TO THEIR PROBLEM AS YOU CAN.)

1. Buy the entire note.
2. Buy the payments only. (They keep the balloon.)
3. Buy the balloon. (They keep the payments.)
4. Buy part of each payment. (They keep the rest.)
5. Buy part of part of the balloon.
6. Buy a fixed number of payments (after you receive yours, they get the rest).
7. Pay par ~ part cash and the balance in some other form.
8. Buy 1/2 of the note now and the other 1/2 at the beginning of the second term.
9. Buy at steep discount now and give the seller the right to buy the note back sometime in the future.
10. Pay par for the note now; but get the right to buy at a discount something else they own (for example: other paper or real estate) sometime in the future.
11. Contract at discount for the note now and agree to make payments on debts or bill they owe as the bills come due until you have used up the contracted price.

12. If all else is failing, try to get an option on the paper for as long as you can, hoping you can find another investor, or the holders will find their problem more pressing than they originally thought.
13. When you have run out of ideas and still cannot make any headway, try this: Write your best offer with a short time-frame for acceptance and depart. (They may call you before the offer runs out.)

SOURCES OF PAPER

Now that you have the basics of Paper and an understanding of negotiating with the sellers, let me point you to some sources of Paper. Here is a list of ideas to help you find real estate secured paper:

* Advertize in your local paper - BUT BE CAREFUL: Check with your lawyer about the laws in your state regarding dealing in Paper.

* Hand out fliers at real estate marketing sessions "HAVE CASH - WANT PAPER."

* Hand out flyers to your local CPAs, attorneys, and real estate offices.

* Talk with hard money lenders (Beneficial Finance) and see if they would like to unload some of their problem loans. (Be sure you can fix the problem before you decide to buy.)

* If you have a friendly real estate broker, look through the available properties offered for sale to see if there are any second mortgages (which will be paid off upon sale). This means some leg work at the registry of deeds. Then get an option to purchase Paper from the holder.

* Create your own Paper by buying improved real estate at discount then sell for cash and paper at retail.

* Acquire a piece of land that can be subdivided into small retail lots for resale. Carry back the owner financing.

* Call on ads advertizing for Paper or Paper for sale. They are a good source to either buy or sell Paper.

* Local business groups are always looking for speakers. Tell them what you do and what you are looking for.

* The key is to get the word out to everyone in your area that you buy real estate secured Paper. Over time, you will get two or three calls a week from people needing to sell their deeds of trusts.

The following list of ideas on cash flows with Paper comes from my one-day seminar, *An Introduction To Paper*.

GENERATING CASH FLOWS WITH PAPER

- Your cash - buy paper.
- Crank (borrow against) assets you own - buy Paper with higher yield.
- Borrow from investors - buy paper with higher yield.
- Borrow from pension funds - buy paper with higher yield.
- Your own IRA account - buy paper.
- Buy asset wholesale - sell at retail for Paper.
- Buy asset with paper - sell retail for cash and paper.
- Ask lenders to discount loans you owe for cash.
- Ask lenders you owe to take other Paper you have bought at discount for payment in full.
- Side-step discount: If a lender won't take other Paper for your debt, buy other Paper at discount and use the income to feed the debt.

- Keep and walk (substitute the security) inexpensive loans (low constant or principal-only) you owe.
- Over-trade discounted Paper in return for assets plus cash.
- Buy REOs from banks with discounted Paper.
- Hypothecate asset you own - buy new asset - sell for cash - take cash and buy discounted Paper.
- Buy S/F house with Paper - rent for positive cash flow.
- Sandwich lease - Rent asset at low rent - re-rent at higher rent - the net cash flow is yours.

LOAN CONSTANTS

One of the most important tools you can have in evaluating any investment with debt is the mathematical structure of that debt. Loan constants will not solve problems, but they will tell you the relationship between the outstanding balance and the debt service. To determine a loan constant for an amortizing loan, you divide the "ANNUAL DEBT SERVICE" (this amount stays the same) by the OUTSTANDING BALANCE OF THE LOAN (this amount gets smaller as the loan amortizes). The answer is expressed as a percentage.

LOAN CONSTANT FORMULA

$$\text{LOAN CONSTANT} = \frac{\text{ANNUAL DEBT SERVICE}}{\text{OUTSTANDING BALANCE}}$$

FOR EXAMPLE:
A CAR LOAN: $10,000 AT 10% FOR 48 MONTHS
MONTHLY PAYMENTS = $253.63 x 12 =
$3,043.51/YEAR (ANNUAL DEBT SERVICE)

MONTHS PAID	BALANCE AT END OF PERIOD	LOAN CONSTANT
0	$10,000.00	30%
12	$ 7,860.18	39%
24	$ 5,496.29	55%
36	$ 2,884.87	105%

*** WHAT IS A GOOD LOAN CONSTANT? ***

As the loan constant gets bigger, the faster the loan is being amortized. But big loan constants eat up the cash flows. So, if you want to free and clear a property quickly, go for a bigger and bigger loan constant. If you are in need of cash flows, soften (make smaller) the loan constant. Measure the loan constant on every debt you have such as mortgages on your home, car loans, student loans, credit card loans and consumer loans. This is a great place to start a Paper portfolio (cash generator) by paying off these high constant loans with available cash or low constant loans. The idea is to pay off the high loan constant debts and not to repeat the process again by getting into more high constant loans. By paying off the high constant debt with softer constant debt, you have increased your monthly cash flows by the difference between the old high debt service and the new lower debt service. However, it is very important to note that you have greatly extended the time period over which you must repay the debt.

When you are studying a note offered for sale, be sure to determine the present loan constant. The bigger it is, the better the yields. And should the payor of the note get in trouble in the future, a big loan constant can be softened to improve his situation to a degree.

Now that you are aware of the important relationship between debt and debt service, I hope you will always analyze each and every debt every time you come across a loan.

YOUR PAPER PORTFOLIO

YOUR PAPER PORTFOLIO

Paper management has always been easy and not very time consuming. With the advent of computers and software designed to keep every conceivable record, there is no excuse for poor record keeping. Even so, I have spent years developing systems that would make the record keeping even easier—even to the point where I figured out a way to have someone pay me to collect and post the payments owed to me.

I use my "record account." This is an interest-bearing checking account set up in a bank near the payor. The account is a personal or business account set up in my name or my company name. I have the sole signature rights and I hold all the checks. The note payor gets the deposit receipts and some pre-paid envelopes supplied by the bank. Each month before his payment is due, the payor mails his payment check with the completed deposit slip to the prescribed bank. The day it receives the deposit by mail the bank mails me a notice of receipt and deposit. I use one bank for up to four deposits (none of which are in the same dollar amount) and then I find another bank willing to do the record keeping. This saves me a lot of grief.

First, I no longer have to endorse the check and somehow remember to get it into a bank account. (At least a day's delay saved.) Secondly, by the time I get the receipt from the bank, the payor's check has just about cleared his bank. Another delay averted. Thirdly, after posting the paid amount to my master payment sheet, I throw the correct deposit receipt into the proper file taken from the drawer marked "due this month" (and each file is in order by dollar amount rather than by payor name). I replace the file in the "paid-this-month" drawer. Very easy to open either drawer to see who has paid and who has not. With everyone paid at the end of the month I change the name of the "paid" drawer to "owed this month" and I am off and running again.

Late payor files wind up on my desk marked "Urgent: Attention Needed." A letter goes out encouraging prompt payment. If that fails I meet with the payor to determine the problem. There are lots of ways to win with sugar. I offer a 10% discount if the payment is in the bank the day it is due. The 10% discount plus compounded interest gets added onto the end of the payment schedule. As you have gathered by now, I have been known to acquire a house or two. Here is an opportunity to offer to cut their monthly payments by half or completely in return for part ownership of their house. Another effective solution, depending upon the talents of the payors, I have traded work credits for partial payment. I have found most people are honest and will pay if they just have the means. It is my belief that somehow we can work it out. Foreclosure is always a "cure." Since 1972, when I first started buying discounted Paper, I have not yet instituted foreclosure.

Whatever method of record keeping you choose, it is best to start with the first note you acquire. Keep it simple, logical and easy to do every month or things tend to get out of control quickly. Computers, one of which is staring back at me at this very moment, are wonderful once you become "computer friendly." We older folk seem to have an aversion for them. Kids have absolutely no fear of them and can really make them sing. Get one of your kids to set up your record keeping account. He will learn about the wonderful world of Paper and you will learn that computers can be user friendly.

Remember to set up an amortization schedule of your cost basis in each note you purchase. Otherwise you will be spending your capital and not know it. Every month I add up all my principal recapture from all notes and move it by check to a special account. There, it is ready to acquire another note when the opportunity arises. Keep your interest totals ready for your CPA. All that interest is taxable somehow somewhere.

The key to record keeping is to start early in the game and understand your system so that it will give you bottom lines every month and annually on the balances owed to you, your principal recapture position, your interest income and your tax liability.

MORE IDEAS ABOUT HOLDING PAPER: Yes, Paper generates cash flows and profits through discount earned. Often the yields can get surprisingly high even after tax. But the problem with Paper is that there is no growth in the Paper itself. Let me point out a couple of areas where Paper is a real power house. First, Paper income (or for that matter, income from any source) held in pension plans, KEOGHs, and IRAs is not taxed until the funds are withdrawn from the account. Without the tax impact, Paper in these plans gets interesting fast. Look into "self-directed" IRAs - there are a few banks which will accept a self directed plan. Put some of your Paper into these plans and watch the growth.

Another means of getting some growth out of Paper it to use the net cash flows (the interest portion of your monthly note payments) to help fund your real estate acquisition and holding programs. For example, you have three rental houses that are and will be short of making their monthly payments by $150.00 per month for the next year or two. By then the rents should catch up to necessary outgo. In the meantime you can fund this negative cash flow ("eat") out of a savings account or invest in a discounted note which will throw off more than enough interest to cover the eat. In this way your investment houses don't erode your capital and the income stream from them will continue even after the houses are on an even footing.

Another method is to get an option on a note which you then trade as a down stroke on a distressed single family house. The small income stream from the note you negotiated at deep discount might really appeal to a house owner who is in deep trouble. You'll never know unless you ask. Once all parties are in agreement, going to settlement steps are easy. Take your cash and close on the discounted note. Take the note and assign it to the house owners for a deed to their house. Record the necessary documents and you are done. You have put some growth into Paper through your use of real estate and Paper.

There are many ways to combine existing Paper with real estate to resolve all kinds of problems. A real working knowledge of Paper is absolutely essential if you ever hope to fully understand real estate investing. A knowledge of ways to properly divest yourself of your Paper from time to time is as essential as knowing how to acquire and manage your Paper. Let me describe divestiture briefly and then we'll move on to case studies.

DIVESTITURE OF PAPER

DIVESTITURE

As I have discussed before, Paper generates cash flows and is a source of potential profit through the discount acquired at the time of purchase. The amount of the discount you achieved at the time of purchase will grow smaller with each payment received. This is because the monthly payment must be broken into two parts: the first being the interest or "yield" (this is the taxable portion of the payment) paid on the outstanding balance of your invested capital and the remaining portion of the payment is the partial recapture of your initial purchase price (your invested capital). The actual dollar amount of your interest or "profit" each month will decrease as the loan is amortized. If your main source of income is from discounted Paper cash flows, then be sure to reinvest your recaptured principal as often as you can in solid, reliable Paper with reasonable yields. This effort on your part will keep your cash-flow levels from diminishing to unacceptable levels. DO NOT SPEND YOUR CAPITAL - REINVEST IT WISELY!!!

If you hold "interest-only" notes you have no capital recapture to worry about and your bookkeeping is very easy. The problem is, with no debt reduction by the payor each month, the payor is facing a balloon which might not be manageable in tight money times. Also, another potential problem with non-amortizing loans is the lack of principal pay down within the note and security instrument. Thereby any equity build up in the property comes from appreciation in market value. When property values level off or fall as they have in the past three years, some note holders (including many banks) find themselves owed more than the property is worth. This situation can bring about a sense of nervousness among note holders. If you are in need of the cash flows from Paper, there is no need to consider divestiture except in the case of problem payors. Rectify the situation as quickly as possible—time will only cost you money.

One final point. It is better to have many little notes than one big one. Don't put all your eggs in one basket.

If cash flow from Paper is not your major income source, then you are in a position to be more aggressive with your existing Paper. There are numerous ways to increase your yield and realize your profit in paper after you have acquired it. To increase yields requires some or all of these elements: time, effort, negotiating skills, patience, other sources of capital, an in-depth knowledge of transaction structuring, an extensive knowledge of documentation mechanics, and creativity. Below is a list of ways to increase post-purchase yields. Where necessary, I will go into some detail in the "cases" section.

INCREASING YIELDS WITH PAPER YOU HOLD

*** Cause prepayment by the payor.

*** Offer the payor a small discount to buy back his note.

*** Increase the yield by cutting the interest rate and increasing the payment with a cooperative payor.

*** Sell all of the note at a lower yield to recover your capital and part of the discount earned.

*** Sell part of the Paper at a lower yield to recover part of your capital - retain part ownership - continue to receive part of the payments.

*** Pay off loans you owe with your Paper acquired at discount.

*** Trade good Paper for bad, provided you have a sure solution for the problem situation.

*** Trade good Paper for discounted REOs held by banks.

*** Add cash to your note to buy something else at discount.

*** Over-trade your Paper for cash and real estate.

*** Pledge your Paper as security for a note with soft terms to buy real estate - sell the real estate for cash - reinvest the cash in more discounted Paper.

*** Trade your Paper for an option on a s/f house for future growth and profit.

*** Trade your Paper for part or all of the ownership of a s/f house.

*** Paper and "must take" - offer to sell good note if buyer will take a problem note or property off your hands. The Paper may have been a good investment; but the "problem" was costing you more than you were making on the good Paper.

PAPER CASE STUDIES

CASE: PIECES OF PAPER

SITUATION: An existing note: $10,000 original balance, 10% interest, 15 year term, direct reduction, with 5 year balloon; balance at end of 5 years will be $8,132.00, paying $107.46 per month.

PROBLEM: You would like to invest in the note, but at this time you do not have enough money to purchase the entire note.

PROPOSED SOLUTION:
If you break the note up into its parts you might find a way to buy part now and the rest later. Split it up as follows:

A. At 18% yield the entire note would cost $7,560.

B. At 18% yield the 60 monthly payments only, without the balloon, would cost $4,232 today.

C. At 18% yield the balloon only in 60 months would cost $3,328 today.

BENEFITS:
By looking at and analyzing each part of a series of income streams, you, as an investor, will find many different ways to acquire pieces of a note depending upon the needs of the seller and your own needs at the time of negotiation.

CASE: PURCHASE-OPTION BACKS

"*In its simplest form, an Option is the right of one party in a transaction to keep an offer open which has been made by another party in the transaction.*" Quoted from Jack Miller.

BENEFITS OF OPTIONS

1. Minimal management
2. High leverage
3. Low risk
4. Allow for a larger portfolio
5. Larger investment yields
6. Avoid most alienation clauses
7. Provide a great deal of present and future flexibility
8. Used to have favorable tax treatment
9. Optionee has very low (invisible) financial profile
10. Difficult to attach legally when structured properly

In Massachusetts in 1974, I began buying Paper with Purchase-Option Backs (POBs). The yields were impressive. Back then, in almost all states, it was legal for one party to sell an asset at deep discount and take back an option for the right to repurchase the asset at a later date. Times and laws have changed.

BE ABSOLUTELY CERTAIN YOU GET EXPERT LEGAL ADVICE REGARDING PURCHASE-OPTION BACKS. There have been problems with both real estate and Paper. I have included them here in the manual for two reasons: First, if the use of POBs turns out to be legal in your state, you have a wonderful technique with which to solve problems. I have been both a buyer and a seller of POBs and never had a problem at any time with any of the transactions. Second, if usury laws or any other law in your state prohibit the use of POBs, then you need to know what one looks like, feels like and smells like, so you won't step on one. CAUTION AND LEGAL COUNSEL ARE THE KEYS HERE.

CASE: THE POB (PURCHASE-OPTION BACK) FORMULA

SITUATION: $10,000 note, 10% interest only (paid monthly), with a balloon in 5 years. The note is 12 payments old.

PROBLEM: Holder need to raise cash with the note, but a straight sale at discount proves to be too great a loss of equity to the holder.

PROPOSED SOLUTION:
Use the POB Formula.

Offer 50 cents (negotiable) on the dollar of the face amount with the option for the seller of the note to repurchase his $10,000 note back at any time (negotiable) over the life of the loan for 50 cents (negotiable) on the dollar.

BENEFITS:

Seller gets necessary cash ($5,000) and has the option back to repurchase the note even if the note is prepaid.

Buyer has a safe investment yield of 20%.

In all the numerous POBs I have done, only one did not exercise his option.

The Agreement I use is on the next page.

REVIEW THE FOLLOWING WITH LEGAL COUNSEL BEFORE EVER ATTEMPTING ITS USE.

AGREEMENT

WHEREAS, ____
(SELLER) is the owner of a note in the face amount of $_________________________
For ______ years with a stated interest rate of _______ percent per annum, which note is dated ___________________________ and payable to said Seller from the Payors,

____

Said note being secured by a Deed of Trust of even date recorded in the County of _________________, State of _____________, Registry of Deeds in Book _____ Page _____ and

WHEREAS _________________________________(BUYER) wishes to purchase said note and Deed of Trust and the said

____(Seller) desires to sell said note to the Buyer,

NOW, THEREFORE, it is hereby mutually agreed by and between the parties as follows:

1. The Buyer shall pay the sum of $_____________________ for said note and Deed of Trust, which note and Deed of Trust shall be assigned by recordable assignment this day to the said Buyer and the said Seller shall direct the Payor of said note to make all payments which are due and payable from this day forward to the Buyer.

2. It is hereby agreed by and between the parties that the Seller shall have the right, as long as said note is not in default, to purchase the said note and Deed of Trust at any time upon the payment of $_______________ plus any unpaid payments then due to the then holder in due course.

In the event said note is in default, Buyer shall notify the Seller in writing that said note is in default and the Seller shall have the right to:

a. bring the payments current and correct the default within ten days of written notification, or

b. purchase said note in the manner prescribed in Paragraph Number 2 in the above, or

c. abandon his option to purchase said note and relinquish all rights and all claims to any interest whatsoever in the said note and Deed of Trust.

This AGREEMENT becomes null and void fifteen days after the Seller is notified, in writing, by the holder that the note is in default. The Seller must notify the holder in due course in writing which of the three above-stated options (a, b, or c)Seller intends to perform within the stated fifteen day period.

IN WITNESS WHEREOF, the parties have hereunto set their hands and seals the _____ day of ____________, 19_____.

________________________	________________________
(SELLER)	(BUYER)

CASE: POB - DIRECT REDUCTION NOTES

SITUATION: The Note $3,625 - created today; 6% interest; 36 monthly payments; direct reduction; payable $110.28 per month (P + I).

PROBLEM: Holder needs cash in a hurry for another deal in which he feels he can make a quick profit.

POTENTIAL SOLUTION: POB (PURCHASE-OPTION BACK)
Purchase for 50 cents on the dollar with an option to the seller to repurchase the note back during the term of the for 50 cents on the then outstanding balance.

BENEFITS:
Fast cash to the note holder
Note seller can exercise his option to purchase note
High cash-flow yield to the investor
Excellent double security

CASE: CAUSING PREPAYMENT

SITUATION: I had purchased a $6,000 note of which 7 months had been paid. The payments were $59.90 per month and had always been on time. The original note was created on a 20 year amortization schedule with the balance to balloon in 5 years. The stated rate was 10.5%. My purchase price had been $3,300.

The security was a renovated (by the payor) 3 family (owner occupied) in a very nice historic section of Salem, Massachusetts. This was the Payor's situation when he purchased the property:

Property purchase price:	$ 37,000
Bank 1st	$ 25,000
Purchase money 2nd	$ 6,000 (Purchased by me)
Down payment by Payor	$ 6,000

$249.60/month First; $ 59.90/month second; Total: $309.50/month

PROBLEM: Although my yield was 29%, it occurred to me that if I could accelerate the prepayment I would have the discount earned at purchase to reinvest instead of waiting for 53 months.

POTENTIAL SOLUTION:
I met with the payor and showed him the mathematics of where he was at the moment. He immediately understood when I explained to him that he could refinance his existing first up to $36,880 at 9% for 25 years from the same bank. His new payment to the bank would be $309.50 per month - exactly the same he was already paying. The refinancing was easy because the property had been renovated and it was now owner occupied. In a week we were both at the closing in the bank.

BENEFITS:
After paying off the old 1st ($24,329), the closing costs ($300), and paying off the 2nd ($5,840) which I had owned for one month, the payor put what was left ($6,411) of the refinancing proceeds happily into his pocket. This was a good deal all the way around.

CASE: INCREASE YIELD - PASSIVE INVESTOR'S CASH & YOURS

SITUATION: New note $11,000, well secured, at 13-3/4%, paying $225.19 per month for 72 months. Note can be bought to yield 30% at a cost of $7,400.

PROBLEM: How to increase the yield

POTENTIAL SOLUTION:
A friend, who is a passive investor and understands the numbers, says he can live with 24% return if you will take care of all the details (subject to his review). He will put up $5,400 if you will put up $2,000.

Investor's position is $5,400 invested at 24% per year for 72 months and receive $142.16 per month.

Your position is $2,000 invested to receive 72 monthly payments of $83.03 ($225.19 - $142.16 = $83.03). Your yield is 46.6%.

BENEFITS:

Investor gets well secured 24% return managed by you. You have increased your return substantially.

CASE: INCREASE YIELD - CUT THE RATE AND INCREASE THE PAYMENT

SITUATION: Yesterday you purchased a note at discount. Original terms were $3,500 at 12% for 84 months. There are now 60 payments remaining. Payments are $61.78. You paid $2,000 and your yield is 27.6%.

PROBLEM: You wish to increase your yield

POTENTIAL SOLUTION:
Negotiate with the payor. Offer to cut the interest rate from 12% to 6% in return for the payor doubling his monthly payment from $61.78 to $123.56. He agrees. A new amortization schedule is created: Balance owed is $2,777 at 6% with monthly payments $123.56. This will amortize in less than 24 months.

BENEFITS:

Payor: Pays off debt much earlier at a lower rate of interest.

Note holder increases his yield from 27% to 41%

CASE: INCREASING YIELD - CASH AND PAPER FOR PAPER

SITUATION: A note, $9,000, on a schedule 120 payments of $137.05 including 13.5% interest, with a balloon of $5,956.01 in 60 months. Holder feels the note is worth 80 cents on the dollar.

PROBLEM: At this price the yield is slightly over 17% and unacceptable to you.

POTENTIAL SOLUTION:
Try offering $8,000 to be paid as follows: $3,000
cash now and a note back to the seller for $5,000
due and payable to the seller of the note when the note balloons.

BENEFITS:
Seller of the note gets 89 cents on the dollar with $3,000 cash now and $5,000 cash when the note
pays off, Buyer gets cash flow and an excellent
yield (51.8%)

CASE: TRADE GOOD PAPER FOR BAD PAPER

SITUATION: Individual sold a small single family house for $35,000 payable $29,000 proceeds from a new loan and a purchase money second mortgage for $6,000 at 10% for 60 months with monthly payments of $127.48.

PROBLEM: No payments are being made on the 2nd mortgage.

POTENTIAL SOLUTION:
Exchange a good note you hold - $3,000 - 9% - $50.00/ month in terest only for the above described non-paying note.

Renegotiate the payment schedule of the non-paying payor. Change the monthly payments from $127.48 per month to $50.00 per month for 36 months and then a balloon.

BENEFITS:
Bad note Payee gets good paying note.
Bad payor gets payments reduced by $77.48 which he can now manage.

You give 80 payments of $50.00 per month and receive 36 payments of $50.00 and a $6,000 balloon.

CASE: EXTRACTING CASH FROM PAPER

SITUATION: There is an existing Note, 20 days old, held by a broker in his portfolio. Excellent security with a strong Payor.

The note: $12,000. 10% interest, 10 year direct reduction paying $158.58 per month.

PROPBLEM: Broker needs cash to pay an overdue I.R.S. bill. He calls me to see if I will pay cash for his note in a hurry.

POTENTIAL SOLUTION:
I bought the note for $7,200 cash: to yield 24%
I sold note the same day to a dentist pension plan to yield 16%. Investor paid me $9,567.

BENEFITS:
Original holder received cash and paid the I.R.S.
Investor's pension plan received a well-secured performing note yielding 16%
I received $2,267 cash for understanding the paper market.

CASE: FEEDING YOUR ALLIGATOR

SITUATION: An alligator is anything that eats dollars voraciously. In my case it was a Chevy Blazer Truck (two months old). It was a bank repo which I could buy for $6,000. The book value was $9,000.

PROBLEM: I had no desire to put $6,000 into the Blazer, but I wanted it if I did not have to pay for it.

PROPOSED SOLUTION:
De-fang the Alligator:
Step 1: (Bank #1) Got $6,000 Blazer loan 10.5% 48 mo costing $153.62 per month
Step 2: (Bank #2) Got $9,000 unsecured loan, interest-only 11% $ 82.50 per month
Step 3: Bought $14,000 note with the $9,000 cash from Bank #2. Note was for 9 years direct reduction at 12% paying $212.58 per month.

BENEFITS:
Two banks placed a good loan each.

My position was this:
Bank #1 loan cost (D.R.)
Bank #2 loan cost (I.O.):

Total debt service:
Income from $14,000 discounted note

Cost to own my truck:

$153.62/month $ 82.50/month

$236.12/month

$212.58/month

$ 23.54/month

That was close enough. I now could justify my truck which would cost me under $24.00 per month. At the end of 48 months the Blazer loan had amortized to zero at which time the loan balance due me on the discounted $14,000 note had amortized down to $9,556.51. I assigned the payment to Bank #2(1 still owed them the $9,000 I had used to purchase the discounted note) and they collected the payments until they were paid in full.

SUMMARY

Benjamin Disraeli (1804-1881), the distinguished author and Prime Minister of Great Britain said, "One only learns from one's mistakes, not one's successes." By making more than my share of mistakes, hopefully, I have learned a few things. From these experiences came a desire to share what I learned with others and thus the writing of this first edition. One goal of this writing has been to provide people with some of the ideas and techniques that have been a very essential part of my life for twenty-five years. Another objective has been to prove to myself that I could write it.

Finally, out of it all, come a couple of essential points. Your ability, or lack of it, to build relationships with others which work well for both parties is the absolute essence of anybody's life. Relationships are built and strengthened through the art of counseling. Practice counseling (questioning and listening and thinking) and improve your skill every day.

The other essential point - be as educated and brilliant as you can at everything you choose to do. Be the smartest kid on the block at whatever you do by always seeking to learn more. Set aside two hours each day for your continuing education program. Study anything and everything that interests you and will help you reach your goals in life. Take it from this expert, "If you think education is expensive, try ignorance." Set up a plan to achieve your goals and work the plan.

D E V E L O P A P L A N

Develop a plan

to focus, evaluate and set your goals
to continually upgrade your skills and knowledge
to manage your physical and emotional resources.
to properly and orderly use your time
to expand and improve all your relationships
to reach your goal and to be happy on the way to those goals
to enjoy every minute of this life.

WORK YOUR PLAN.

Finally, thank you, to all my mentors and friends all over this country. Each of you knows the deep gratitude I have for all you have done. Without you, I never could have survived nor would I have wanted to.

My very best to you,

P. Thorpe

Made in the USA
Monee, IL
13 September 2026

62979549R00100